AN ANCIENT PATH

Public Talks on Vipassana Meditation
as taught by S. N. Goenka
given in
Europe and America
2007

by
Paul R. Fleischman, MD

VIPASSANA RESEARCH PUBLICATIONS ✧ ONALASKA, WA, USA

VIPASSANA RESEARCH PUBLICATIONS
an imprint of

Pariyatti Publishing
867 Larmon Road, Onalaska, WA 98570
www.pariyatti.org

ISBN: 978-1-928706-52-6 (E-Book)

ISBN: 978-1-928706-53-3 (Print)

Library of Congress Control Number: 2009921669

With special thanks to TSJZ and DMT

*At last I have become old enough
to have young people to teach me.*

Contents

Preface

The talks collected in this book were given to varying audiences under unique circumstances that partly shaped what was said. I hope some of the pleasant ambience of these occasions comes over in print.

This is not a collection of essays. The talks stand side by side, all having the same center, which is reached from a different angle each time. The Boston talk was to mental health professionals in the USA. The Freiberg talk was given to "Mindfulness" researchers in Germany. The Madrid talk was given in a hospital, with a translator, that slowed and limited its length. Before the Vienna talk, I was advised to speak as if the audience had a pre-existing, intellectual knowledge of Buddhism, and I was asked to specifically address the topic of "Karma and Chaos." Before the Dublin talk I was admonished to give a literary and intellectual cast to the presentation. In Ghent I was asked to speak to a University audience with a more philosophical background.

To me each talk was a memorable mingling with new places and people, and an echo of dozens of other talks that either were never recorded, or that lacked anything specifically different enough to be worth presenting alongside of what is written here. Because every introductory talk, regardless of the angle of approach, has to cover some similar material, not all talks are worth saving, and there is a lot of repetition in this book. Much of the repetition has been preserved, so that the talks remain in themselves generally coherent and intact, but since all audio files were edited for readability, the written word varies significantly from audio material bearing the same title and date.

I would suggest that the talks be read one at a time, and the book (or computer screen) closed in between for a while. When it is reopened, I hope the next talk will have enough that is new to sound vivid and fresh, and enough repetition of essentials to have the effect of a chorus.

The Garden Cottage
Bloomington, Indiana July 2008

We can annex every age to ours...all of those distinguished founders of holy creeds were born for us and prepared for us a way of life...nature allows us to enter into a partnership with every age...I have surrendered myself to wise men...So if you devote to your studies the time you have taken from public duties, you will not have deserted nor evaded your task...for the soldier is not the only man who stands on the battle line...we have gone out to have dealings with the whole earth and claim the world as our country...

Seneca
Translation by C.D.N. Costa

A Way of Life

*An Address to the Harvard Medical School
Department of Continuing Education
Boston, Massachusetts
June 1 – 2, 2007*

When meditation first crossed the boundaries of Asia and began to have a significant impact upon the Western world thirty to forty years ago, most of the people who were transporters of this cultural exchange were young adults, who were seeking something new that would help to transform themselves and the culture they had been left with. In the 1960's and 70's, World War II and Vietnam still were casting a long shadow over daily life. In the mid 1990's, twenty-five years along into this flowering of cultural exchange, there was a cartoon in the *New Yorker* magazine showing a guru sitting in solitude surrounded by Himalayan peaks. There are huge, cartoonishly sharp mountains behind him. The guru is lean and bony, clearly not dining on McBurgers, and dressed only in a loincloth, and with very long hair and a beard trailing below his navel onto the ground. Climbing up towards him, clambering upward by his fingertips, is another cartoon character you could describe as "an aging hippy." He has long hair pulled back in a ponytail, but the top of this head is bald and he has gray hair. He has a very beaten up old backpack that was first seen in Katmandu in 1971. The guru looks down on the aging hippy scrambling up towards him, and says: "Frankly, I was hoping to attract a younger audience."

That does not pertain today. I am glad to see an audience peppered with gray hair. One of the signs that meditation has taken root in the West is that it is no longer confined to any social, cultural, or generational pocket. People of any age, of any ethnicity, or of any background have found it acceptable and are interested in it.

I would like to begin talking about meditation as a way of life by making it clear that meditation is not a treatment. Of course there are some interrelationships with psychotherapeutic treatments that I will address later. But meditation is a bigger and broader activity than the professional treatment of illness and dysfunction.

Here in Massachusetts we ought to start by paying deference to Henry David Thoreau. This glittering high-rise hotel in which we are meeting today is only a handful of miles from the small town and woodlots and little rivers and ponds he made sacrosanct in and around Concord. Thoreau was one of the first Americans to gain access to the Asian texts, both Hindu and Buddhist, which were coming out of the British Empire in the early part of the Nineteenth Century. Most Americans were unaware of these books and the ideas they contained, but Thoreau was well networked to a few English intellectuals, who shipped these translations across the Atlantic to him. We typically read *Walden* in high school as the quintessentially American experience of nature and wilderness in the New World. In fact, Thoreau explicitly says he was attempting to reproduce what he imagined to be—based upon his reading—the methods of Indian lifestyle meditators. If you re-read *Walden* carefully you will see that he repeatedly praises Asian literature and the culture that produced it, as exemplary of the contemplative life. He created the sojourn at Walden Pond in order to partake of the Asian experience of a meditative lifestyle. He said that only from his days in solitude near Walden Pond did he come to "…realize what the Orientals mean by contemplation…" that due to his own artesian experiences the water of Walden had now mingled with the Ganges, and that the visions within Indian texts exceeded and improved the constricted concepts of the West. Thoreau says in the chapter, "Where I Lived and What I Lived For," "I went to the woods to live deliberately, to front only the essential facts of life, and see if I could not learn what it had to teach, and not, when I came to die, discover that I had not lived .... and be able to give a full account of it in my next excursion." Without even bothering to justify or elaborate that famous comment, Thoreau poked his walking stick through the fabric of Western thought, and affiliated himself with the Indian tradition of invoking rebirth as an inspiration for living well in this birth. Was he just being playful or ironic?

Inspired by people like Thoreau, about thirty-five years ago I returned to India, which I had originally visited as a medical student. I returned to find, study, and practice meditation. At that time I began a meditation practice, which I continue to this day, called Vipassana meditation. My teacher at that time and still today is Mr. S. N. Goenka. The word "Vipassana" is a Pāli word, which has now become incorporated into English. Pāli is a language of ancient India, a spoken colloquial form of Sanskrit. Sanskrit was the classic literary language, which retained its literary position but eventually disappeared from spoken usage. Pāli was a spoken street language and Vipassana was preserved in what was then an accessible tongue. Vipassana means, seeing realistically. So Vipassana meditation was differentiated from the other forms of meditation that were common 2,500 years ago in India by the fact that it was supposed to be approachable by the common man and to be entirely realistic. It was not supposed to be in the possession of any ethnic or political group, nor to require priests or professional expertise to be put into practice. It had no religious, philosophical or ideological trappings. It was a realistic meditation for the ordinary person.

I took my first ten-day Vipassana course in India in 1974, and the exact same course that I took then is available today at the Vipassana Meditation Center in Shelburne Falls, Massachusetts. I would like to describe to you how Vipassana is taught today and how this teaching is linked to its ancient roots. Vipassana is taught as a path, that is to say as a lifestyle, or way of life. Maybe in psychiatric terminology you could say, "a lifestyle intervention." It has the atmosphere you find in Thoreau's writing, in which life is focused on appreciation, intensity and activity.

I emphasize the word, "activity" because to some extent, as meditation entered the Western world, those of it's pioneering early students who were mental health professionals kept their meditation practice somewhat closeted. Their caution to reveal that they were meditators—particularly if they were psychiatrists, psychologists, or other psychotherapists—was realistic prudence. Meditation had been stereotyped in the West as a mildly contemptible form of escapism and passivity. I know that these stereotypes actually existed and were not just figments of the imaginations of the early generation of Western meditators… because I myself held them. Meditation was loaded down with a lot of negative baggage. Freudians would tell you that it was merely seeking an "oceanic experience," which was a regressive wish to fuse with the memory of the mother. Activists said it was self-satisfaction and reneging on the obligation to improve society. Cynics pointed out how silly and shallow it seemed to them that the Beatles or Mia Farrow purchased meditation like a new marketing strategy for their images. Meditation was seen as a gimmicky product of shyster gurus. People who meditate were said to just sit around staring at their navels. So, like many others, I was leery and skeptical along with being intrigued. I was quite ambivalent. I wanted to learn about meditation but I didn't want to become an ineffectual person. After World War II and the Holocaust, who could imagine a merely passive and sedative life as being either ethical or survivable? I wanted peace and harmony, but not at the expense of competence or of vivid and responsible living.

Our Nineteenth Century Massachusetts exemplar, Thoreau, was a Harvard graduate, a surveyor, a manufacturer, a businessman, a teacher, as well as a writer. So I emphasize the word, "activity" in order to show that my original concern about being duped or psychologically lobotomized, which was and maybe is shared by many other people, is 180 degrees wrong. If we think of Thoreau as a local founder of meditation as a way of life, we should be reminded of the appreciation with which he experienced every moment, the vigor and hardiness of his outdoor existence, and the intensity with which he engaged social and political responsibilities. When he died, Thoreau was more eulogized as an abolitionist, a fan of John Brown's courage and commitment to end slavery, an antagonist to the politics of compromise, and a conductor on the Underground Railway, than he was as a literary figure.

A Vipassana course today is always taught in a ten-day format. If you want to learn Vipassana in its authentic, unmodified tradition, you need to be able to take ten days of your life and go to a ten-day residential course. There may be many reasons why Vipassana requires ten days of residential learning but I want to focus your attention on the most important one. Vipassana means meditating on reality, but it also more specifically means meditating on reality in an unbroken, continuous way. To learn what Vipassana really offers, you need to give yourself time to meditate morning, noon, evening; morning, noon, evening; morning, noon, evening. You meditate when you are hungry and when you are eating and when you are finished eating, when your stomach is full, when your stomach is empty, when your stomach is full again, when your stomach is empty again. You meditate when you are waking up, when you are newly awakened, when you are fully awake, when you are sleepy after lunch, when you are awake in the afternoon, when you are sleepy in the evening, learning to meditate through all the different stages of satiety and wakefulness.

This is critical because it differentiates meditation from any artificial, idealized state. If you learn to meditate in a particular way, at a particular time of day, in a particular posture or physical or mental condition, you develop the idea that *this* is what meditation really is. But actually, that would be one extracted parenthesis from your life. It would be an ideal period of life that you had set aside very thoughtfully to meditate. However, meditation on reality has to be unbroken over periods of time because reality is constantly changing. The conditions of your life are constantly changing. If your meditation is available to you only in idealized states, then the very times that you would most like to be able to access meditation, for example under distress, under exhaustion or agitation, meditation will be unfamiliar to you. But if you launch your practice of meditation under a continuous cycle of days in which all your physical and mental states appear in front of you, then your initial learning brings meditation to bear under a wide variety of personal experiences without selecting out and claiming only one state as meditation. You learn to meditate under many of the conditions that your mind and body will present to you.

A ten-day Vipassana course begins with a series of vows. The vows are not taken to placate someone else. No one is going to be monitoring your brain waves to see whether you are keeping your vows or not. The vows are taken by yourself, to yourself, as an orienting process by which you start yourself off in the right direction. You inculcate in yourself the right attitudes to meditate. The first important vow is that of Noble Silence. Nine of the ten days are spent entirely in Noble Silence. Noble Silence means that you are actually encouraged to talk when speech is contributory to meditation, that is to say, when speech is Noble: for example, when you are discussing your practice with your teacher, or when you need to discuss a management issue with volunteer staff, like having forgotten to pack toothpaste in your suitcase. Noble Silence means that your intention is to be silent with yourself and with everybody else for any other than essential needs. Noble Silence refers not only to speech but also to gestures and all other activities. For ten days you are asked to refrain from reading, writing, computers, telephone, anything that will call you away from the practice of self-observation. Sometimes people say this sounds hard or scary. But to me, if there were nothing else to a ten-day course than Noble Silence, that would be the greatest thing. I emblemize it by saying: "Ten days without having to answer a single phone call!" You finally can tell all the annoyances of modern life to wing it, and you give one hundred per cent of yourself to learning something new and valuable.

The second set of vows are the five moral vows that are familiar to anybody from any tradition around the world, not to kill, not to steal, not to lie, not to use intoxicants, and not to commit sexual misconduct, which for the purpose of a ten-day course means to be celibate. Whether you come alone or with a spouse or friend, men and women are separated and you live by yourself within yourself. Each person is autonomous. The intention of these vows is to focus all your volition on maintaining as continuous meditation as you can muster throughout the cycle of the days.

And then you take a vow to follow the teaching as it is given, without adding to it or subtracting from it. This is important because people come for ten days and sometime on the third or fourth or fifth day when they might be facing some minor point of confusion or doubt or frustration they may think to themselves, "Why don't I just start doing the kind of meditation that I have done previously, or that soothing technique I read about, or the prayer that I learned when I was a child," and of course that could lead to massive confusion. You've been alone in the silence of your mind but being given clear and specific guidance and suddenly you start deviating from this guidance and you produce a mental mess, a psychic ratatouille. To prevent this you are asked to take a vow to follow the master chef's recipe for ten days. This is simply giving the teaching of Vipassana a fair trial to reveal itself as it is, without your diluting or diminishing it in any way. There is enough spice in it already, I can assure you, so you won't need to flavor it with your home grown garlic.

The course starts with three days of watching the breath. Each day the directions become slightly more specific and detailed so I am only presenting an overview of the general pattern of meditation over the first three days. The exercise of watching your breath reminds me of an episode I had in childhood where you go to a beach and there is a large beach ball and the challenge is: "Stand on top of the beach ball!" The exercise of watching your breath is similar to the exercise of trying to stand on top of a beach ball. As soon as you get on it you fall off. There is a bit of learner's frustration in this but unlike the beach ball, which very few people can actually stand on, there is real growth in the ability to watch your breath.

This exercise of watching your breath, as an introduction to Vipassana, is not intended to just calm you down. The goal of these first three days is mastery of the mind, meaning the ability to say to your mind, "Do this," and your mind obeys you. Most of our life we think we have mastery of our mind. If I am asked to give a talk, I can stand up and give a talk, and when the moderator of this morning's conference holds up a sign that says, "Stop," I will probably stop. We have grossly apparent mastery of the mind. But in the Noble Silence of meditation you realize that subtly your mind is running out of control all of the time.

When we give the mind large externalizing tasks, at that level it is obedient to our intention; but when we give the mind quiet and inflected guidance, it is not used to obeying delicate and nuanced intentions. This is very similar to the free association that Freud observed in which the mind, when released from overweening guidance, runs fluidly from association to association. The mind is constantly moving from topic to topic, from affect to affect, and though we think we are in control of our minds, actually our minds are in control of us, dictating to us from zones beyond our will or intention what we will next think and feel.

The goal of the three days of observing your breath is to be able to give a directive to your mind, "Please attend to breathing," and have the mind follow that directive. So this three-day exercise often begins with frustration but moves gradually towards an improved sense of self-mastery and self-integration, accompanied by feelings of well being, occasionally even some degree of bliss. Most people get some mild degree of the concentration called *samādhi*, the ability to concentrate to the extent that you are temporarily and briefly relieved of the wayward processes of the mind.

Thoreau used a beautiful image that the untrained mind ricochets like a bullet shot in a small room. You want to be able to lessen that lateral and ricochet motion and steer your mind in line with your intention.

The next seven days of the course are given to Vipassana practice proper and the goal of the course changes. The goal is now to obtain a strong experiential root in meditation as you traverse many states of body and mind, to purify your mind of its ignorance and malice, and to allow its wisdom and good-heartedness to gain precedence, predominance, or even exclusive reign. The goal of Vipassana is to sit with yourself through thick and thin, letting go of the problems you generate within your self, and allowing your original and finest volitions to shine. It is a steaming off of the vegetables, a releasing, and at the same time an awakening. In the old days they said things like "letting the lotus open". Today we could say: growth in becoming a brighter router in the network of peace and loving kindness that we would like to get linked up to in this domain or across all domains. Vipassana is intended to give you a faster and more powerful search engine to relocate harmony and shared joy in your archived pages, without having a lot of negative advertising or sleazy web pages cluttering your search results. Learn to Google "awareness" and "equanimity," and guarantee daily email updates, by practicing Vipassana.

The courses are taught in a large meditation hall so you meditate in public in the presence of many people. For much of the day you are free to leave the hall and can also meditate in private, either in your private bedroom, or, if your course is at a meditation center and not just at a temporary camp, you may have a tiny private meditation room. So you meditate in public, in private, hungry, not hungry, sleepy, not sleepy, sad, not sad, happy, not happy, anxious, calm, many, many, many states of mind arising and passing away.

A trademark feature of Vipassana as taught by Mr. Goenka and the Assistant Teachers and Teachers of his lineage is the precise and detailed directions of the teaching. It is not at all free-form trial and error ambiguity. The teaching is very exact. On the morning of day six you are taught to work differently than on the morning of day five. On the evening of day six the directions will change again and so on. Each day you are guided to add a new dimension and a new capacity to your meditation. Of course, there are still enormous periods of time in which you are alone, inside your mind, meditating.

The defining feature of Vipassana is to observe neutrally and realistically the mind-body junction manifested in the sensations of the body. I want to focus your attention on why the sensations of the body become the crux of Vipassana meditation. This will help you understand the actual psychological mechanisms by which Vipassana works, as well as why Vipassana is such a useful tool for a lifestyle of meditation.

The experienced meditator—and at the end of ten days everyone is a relatively experienced meditator—meditates on all the sensations of the entire body all the time. But the course builds up to this capacity and this experience gradually. On the morning of day four you take a tiny specific area of bodily sensations as the focus of your work. By day five you have expanded to a slow excursion through the entire body, and so forth. Why meditate on the sensations of the body as opposed to any other focus? There are millions of possible ways to just be quiet and calm, observe something and meditate. The importance of sensations is several fold. Partly it goes to the joke in that classic movie of our time, "Annie Hall," in which Woody Allen attends a very posh party in Hollywood and in one of the background scenes a young man rushes over to a telephone and in a state of desperation, yells in anguish and despair, "I've forgotten my mantra!" You can't leave your body sensations at home. For the rest of your life they travel with you. They are with you in the airplane, they are with you when you wake up at night, they are with you all day while you are practicing psychotherapy or any other profession, and they will be with you while you are dying. Body sensations are a culturally neutral, non-sectarian, always available, non-religious, non-ideological, realistic focus.

We are temporary aggregations of minds and bodies that live for a period of time and disappear, and meditation that is realistic is based on observing sensations of the body as they rise and fall and change. This is observing what we really are: dynamic, scintillating, ceaselessly transforming aggregates of tiny things.

One of the most important logical questions that is often asked about Vipassana is: "Why not meditate on the contents of the mind? I came here to learn about my mind, to calm my mind, to understand and develop myself. Why not focus directly on the mind?" and of course there are many meditations that do just that. Later on I will explain how we know the way Vipassana was originally defined and practiced. The term Vipassana properly used refers to meditation on sensations of the body. The principle of this goes back to the saying in ancient India that the finger cannot touch itself. If the mind tries to observe the mind, it will always become involved in self-referential chatter. If you try to observe yourself thinking about something, you will think about that something, or if you are lucky you will think about yourself thinking about that something. But you will not be able to observe it. You will become embedded in it, or become part of it. The mind cannot observe the mind any more than the eye can see itself. Body sensations are the other part of the mind, the other side of the coin, the observable component of psychic life. For every mental state there is a corresponding physical state, and for every physical state there is a specific mental correlate.

This used to be difficult to explain to psychotherapists. In the past, all of us had, as I had, a very cognitive training, verbal and psychoanalytically derived. But today, due to our courageous colleagues who have worked so hard to study and to treat trauma, we all recognize that trauma becomes embedded in the body. When people have been traumatized you can say to them, "Look, you have been home from Vietnam for thirty years; there are no helicopter gun ships bursting into fire, there is no enemy penetrating behind American lines here in Amherst, Massachusetts. Why are you so terrified?" The combat trauma veteran, or the woman suffering from trauma after rape, know perfectly well and are in touch with the same reality we are. They know there is no logical reason to fear all day, day after day, for years. But their fear is embedded inside their body, inside the sensations of their body. Memory is in the body as much as it is in the mind. I think as mental health professionals we can all safely say that we live in the era in which mind-body dualism is no longer a tenable theory. Mind and body are two aspects of a simultaneous, synthesizing, multidimensional reality.

When you meditate systematically and continuously on the sensations of your body it is a most remarkable and amazing awakening.

Now here is a point that I would like to emphasize: a person who meditates day after day after day, trying to focus their mind on the sensations of their body, thinking no doubt, forgetfully daydreaming no doubt, but constantly making an effort to return attention to the body and the body only, will, paradoxically but inevitably, be put in touch with mental contents that are revelatory and revolutionary. It is not just trauma that is stored in the body. Wisdom is stored in the body. Calm is stored in the body. Peace is stored in the body. All ideologies are stored in the body. All fears, all ignorance, everything that we call good and bad in ourselves is stored in the body. We are bodies just as much as we are minds. All of us can be located, brought to life, met, understood, in our bodies, if and when our mind perseveringly, sensitively, and continuously travels through the body's sensations. Where the mind contacts the body, the mind-body junction, there is always three-dimensional existence: sensations, mentations, and insight.

One of the things I like to tease our research colleagues about has to do with these trendy publications in which the investigators take a group of meditators and give them an MRI or a CAT scan or some other high tech neuro-imaging analysis while they are meditating, and then the researchers try to glean some fame by reporting their new discovery that meditation changes the brain. I think Harvard is one of the places that seems to be most enthusiastic about these alleged research discoveries. I want to ask the scientists, "Where did you think meditation was occurring? On the other side of the room? Inside of the pet dog?" Of course it is in the body. And of course it includes the brain. And of course some parts of the brain, and of the body, will be more lit up by this activity than other parts . . . for any one interval of observational time. The trouble with neuro-imaging studies is that they are not simultaneously studying the heart, the lungs, the adrenals, the pituitary, the skin, the soles of the feet, the entire integrated organism. If scientists eventually do such a study, they will find that meditation occurs just as much in the soles of the feet or in the adrenal glands as it does in the brain.

When you practice systemic, deep, focused, ongoing meditation on the sensations of the body, you begin to open up to your whole self. You discover your unconscious. This is not merely the Freudian unconscious about your relationships in early childhood, but it includes all the previously unconscious thoughts and feelings that are stored in that body. All of these rise and become exposed at the surface of the mind. Everybody who takes a ten-day Vipassana course has a transformative, catalytic, integrative experience.

There is a great phrase in William James' *Varieties of Religious Experience,* in which he refers to "the acute religion of the few", versus "the chronic religion of the many." A ten-day Vipassana course could be analogized to an acute religious experience as opposed to routinized attendance at repetitive religious rituals. Of course that is only an analogy. Vipassana is not a religion at all. It is a very rewarding psychological experience.

The ten-day course is hard. It requires discipline, tenacity, hard work, and a little bit of courage that goes with self-honesty. Realistically, we have to say this is not for everyone. Even though it is so challenging, the fact remains that it is extraordinary fun. Not simple playful fun, but the kind of fun that appeals particularly to people who are interested in the mind. It is a Safari into your own psychological Serengeti, ceaselessly interesting and full of unexpected beasts. And the hundreds of thousands of people who have taken such courses in the past three decades under the guidance of Mr. Goenka and his lineage are not exceptional people, not talented athletes or intellectuals, but ordinary, undistinguished, average folks. So you can do it! Even I did.

The ten-day course is not just an experience; it is a reorganizing and transformative experience. In 1988 after I took a thirty-day course in India, one of my friends who is a distinguished literary figure in one of India's regional languages, picked me up after the course, and asked me, "Did you have any experiences?" In India this is a colloquial phrasing meaning, did you have any supernatural or otherworldly experience? Did you have a face-to-face conversation with your dead grandmother? Did you feel that you entered a different plane of existence? Did you have a manifestation of the God, Krishna, come to you? So I told her, "No. I didn't have any 'experiences.'" And she was very disappointed and decided that Vipassana must be a waste of time.

Although we have deep, profound experiences in Vipassana, the goal is not just to have narcissistic excitement of the self within the self. The goal is not to make you feel very special, important, a personal favorite of the gods. In fact, experiences that are reorganizing and transformative occur. Their value rests upon whether they are truly transformative. A person who was afraid of something is no longer afraid of it. A person who repressed some of their past experiences may not be so blocked from that memory. A person who has lost touch with parts of themselves may recover lost aspects of themselves.

Most people, most of the time, are not suffering from traumatic sequelae. They simply re-contact the fullness of themselves. That is a gift. Instead of a mind hiding somewhere up in a brain that hovers above a body, we come to feel like a vibrating, interconnected field, a mind-body zone of instant messaging. You know better who you are. You are more truly yourself. When you look at our Vipassana centers around the world you see that we are constantly expanding our capacity for students.

There are Vipassana centers in most of the major countries of the world, throughout Europe, Asia, Latin America, Africa. As soon as the center is built it is hard for the student to get accommodation and the spaces are filled in advance. Probably the number one reason for the enthusiasm with which people greet Vipassana is the sense of contact with the wholeness of oneself. You don't meet Krishna on some other plane of existence. You meet yourself and get to know him or her as you really are.

But these experiences are more than transformative. They are also organizing. Your life can now take new shape. You start living something, which can be called "walking the path." You can become organized around living a way of life that is informed by Vipassana. Vipassana becomes a compass. As you walk the path you want to know whether you strayed to the right or to the left, and by meditating you contact the organizing, direction-giving qualities of the practice to which you can return twice a day for the rest of your life.

You have to keep meditating if you want meditation to continue to be valuable to you. You may well become reorganized to meditate morning and evening. Through meditation you begin to experience yourself as the causative agent, as the responsible executive in the design of your life. You are kept attuned to the linkage between thought, experience and conduct. The way you make choices, the way you use your body, influences your mind, and the way you use your mind influences your body. Your life begins to revolve around the realization of Karma.

Karma is a concept that has been greatly misunderstood and even abused. It is popularly misunderstood to mean fate. Karma rightfully means the opposite of helplessness and fatalism. Karma is a term that is intended to awaken you to the power of volitional choice, which is activated in every second. Every second a person is free to choose. You can't choose everything or anything. You can't choose to be a basketball star who earns $4,000,000 a year. You can't choose to be shortstop on the Red Sox. You can't choose to bring peace to planet Earth. But every moment is a crossroads from which you can walk forward in a different direction.

The way you activate choice is your Karma. Karma means volition or active awareness of how you are going to use the next moment. You can define Karma as continuously reactivated intentional living. This sense of option, opportunity, choice and responsibility is the meaning of Karma. Meditation stirs an intrinsic eagerness to meditate twice a day, to take a meditation course every year, in order to keep developing a sense of well being that comes from the wakefulness, the mindfulness, the consciousness of oneself as the guiding light in one's own life.

We have a question about the way in which meditation is entering our Western world, after having been nurtured in its Asian nest for 2,500 years or more. One of the features of the scientific life that is the hallmark of Western thought, and that is notable in the history of scientific development, and which is responsible for the creation of a scientific community, is the ethos that scientists will honestly refer to the previous publications in their field of study. As scientists, we don't do a study, we don't publish an article, and claim to be the first person ever to think anything like this. No scientific article begins with a sentence: "This is entirely brand new." On the contrary, every scientific article begins: "Here are the precedents, here are the previous studies, here is what the earlier authors wrote." Our integrity, which, our professional journals reinforce by their publication criteria, is based upon the vigor and authenticity of our search to locate in the literature our ancestral thinkers. So it is not the claim to originality that makes the scientist, it is the recognition of the lineage behind the questions being asked. That is why we have the famous aphorism that is attributed to Newton, that he became great by standing on the shoulders of giants.

For meditation in general and for Vipassana in specific we have a written record that goes back 2,500 years, so if you are referring to Vipassana you want to have some idea of what is in that ancient literature. If someone says they are teaching Vipassana, are they adequately informed about and competently referring to the previous literature? For 2,500 years people have been practicing this practice and leaving documentation about what they experienced.

Historically the first use of the word "Vipassana" is in the teachings of the Buddha. "Vipassana" is the name that meditation was given by the Buddha. By Vipassana the Buddha meant: to observe oneself realistically, continuously, and in totality. Vipassana and the teaching of the Buddha stand between two different things with which they are frequently confused. I use the phrase, "the teaching of the Buddha," and not the word, "Buddhism." There was no Buddhism at the time of the Buddha. There was no Buddhism for hundreds of years after the Buddha.

Our teacher, Mr. Goenka, has had Pāli scholars brought to India from countries such as Burma where the study of Pāli is still an active intellectual pursuit. They have completed computer data entry for the Canon in Pāli of the Buddha's teaching. It's many volumes long. Then you can do a coded search for words such as "Buddhism." Neither "Buddhism" nor any equivalent of Buddhism can be found in the teaching of the Buddha. There is no "ism" or philosophy that is attached to the teaching. Instead, he taught a method of meditation which would lead to experiences, which themselves become the guide on the path. One does not become a Buddhist by practicing Vipassana. Buddha wasn't a Buddhist. Mr. Goenka is not a Buddhist. I have not converted to Buddhism. Sometimes people feel leery about beginning the practice of Vipassana thinking, "Well, I am a Hindu, or I'm Jewish, or Catholic, or I'm a staunch Marxist atheist. I don't want to join any other religion, or a new religion, or one that is against my current belief system."

So Vipassana should not be confused on the one hand with Buddhism, but on the other hand it should not be confused with New Age trends. We shouldn't make the mistake of ignoring thousands of years of literature and living tradition. We shouldn't pretend that we know what meditation is unless we are familiar with the practices and the traditions of those who have embodied it across the generations.

In the teaching of the Buddha, Vipassana is walked as a path and it is maintained by "turning the wheel." The simile of turning the wheel means that I rotate a wheel and then I walk away and the rotation will stop due to friction, unless one of you comes up and turns it to keep it rotating. The wheel can turn for as long as someone is willing to come up and give it a spin. The rotation of the wheel is always a voluntary activity. Authentic Vipassana courses are always taught for free. There is no charge for the teaching because the teaching comes from the Buddha. Nobody owns it. There is no one alive who can say they invented it. Nobody can claim it as their personal possession. It is like breathing. We don't charge people for the air, to which we all should have access for free. Although, having stayed overnight in this hotel, I notice that in Boston, it has now become acceptable to charge five dollars for taking a bottle of water out of the in-room refrigerator. So maybe, someday, we will have to pay to breathe. The city of Boston and other great metropolitan areas will capture us and tag us as we come into town and fit us out with little meters over our noses, and when we leave town we will have to pay a tax for every liter of oxygen we have inhaled. But up until now, breathing has been for free and Vipassana has also been for free.

The Buddha gave Vipassana away for free in the same way that trees distribute oxygen into the atmosphere for the benefit of anyone who can breathe.

There are two things that authenticate the true Vipassana tradition. The first thing is that the practice is in line with the description of the teaching of Vipassana that was given by the Buddha. The lineage must be in line with its origins. And the second authenticating point is the teacher-to-student transmission in which the teacher authenticates the knowledge and practice of the student. So the lineage is transmitted both through written historical records and also through non-written, non-verbal, experiential transmission. It is this reception, transmission, and reception that is called turning the wheel. Today there are Vipassana meditation centers all over the world where this authentic transmission has occurred and where the teaching is given away for free.

The question comes up, "If the centers are run for free, then how can they economically continue?" And the answer is that almost everyone who comes to a course appreciates what they have gotten and leaves some donation. No one will ask you for a donation. There will simply be a table with someone sitting there where donations are accepted. This always reminds me of the Appalachian Trail, that beautiful path through the woods running from the American South, at Springer Mountain in Georgia, to Mt. Katahdin in Northern Maine, and now even beyond. Most of us who grow up in the Eastern United States have the opportunity to walk at least a little bit of this fabulous recreational invention. The motto of the Appalachian trial is, "A footpath through the wilderness." But in fact it is not a wilderness at all. It is heavily worked on, designed, built, transformed, cleared, redirected and maintained. As you walk the trail, you walk upon tens of thousands of stones that have been placed in front of you by other people's loving hands as if you were King of the woods and your subjects had come running in front of you to lay out this corridor of granite and gneiss leading two thousand miles through the woods and clearings along the crests of the Appalachian Mountains.

Who pays all these subjects? How can this long collection of stone works, trail shelters, and wooden bridges be paid for? It's all accomplished for free. People have walked the trail, fallen in love with it, and spontaneously been filled with the desire to have subsequent generations walk the trail, pass over the hills, and drink from the streams. Vipassana is a two thousand five hundred year old invisible trail that is maintained by travelers who have had the experience, and who are filled with the wish that others have the opportunity to sweat, toil, step out onto promontories that reveal vistas, and breathe the fresh mountain air. Having walked the path, they rotate the wheel. They have preserved and laid out in front of you the long trail for you to walk for the rest of your life, where you will always be free to wake up to an adventure and to a mountaintop. Your trail guides can give you a guarantee. If you really walk the path, you are guaranteed to want to donate your time and energy to trail maintenance, to insure that others will get the same opportunity. It's that gratifying.

The Appalachian Trail is built in a world of rocks and earth and roots. The path of Vipassana is built in an atmosphere. This is a realm of peace, harmony, non-violence and empathic relatedness with all other living beings, human and non-human. On the one hand, meditation is not a special, magical state of mind, and is the capacity to choicelessly observe the sensations that underpin all states of mind. On the other hand, Vipassana gradually prunes those states of mind that are counter productive to and antagonistic towards the ethos of neutral and equanimous observation. You take out the weeds and find a crop of inner peace.

Non-violence does not mean that a Vipassana meditator needs to take a vow of pacifism, because there are many moral complexities to life. I don't see anyone who is living now or who has ever lived who has the correct answer to each and every particular moral conundrum that we face in our life on earth. The most poignant example of this is the American Civil War. If you say the Civil War was horrible, it killed half a million people, no one should have fought, the soldiers should have resisted, Abraham Lincoln's military draft should have been resisted, then you are saying that you favor the perpetuation of slavery, an institution that was not only not dying out, but was expanding in power, importance, and territory. Obviously if you were a slave you would not be on the same side as the draft resistors. On the other hand, if you embrace the war then you are embracing battles like Gettysburg. During the United States war in Vietnam, approximately 50,000 Americans were killed in combat over a period of about a dozen years. At Gettysburg approximately 50,000 Americans were murdered in three days. So what's the right answer? There is nothing in the teaching of Vipassana that is going to coerce you into making a reduction of reality into one side or another of any vast or overwhelming social issue. Part of the enduring genius of the Buddha's teaching is that he gave ethical guidance without pinning it to situational particulars. The teaching is like geometry class. The textbook gives you the theorem, and you have to apply it to various problems. But the goal of Vipassana is unambiguously pointed towards a lifestyle in which you continuously seek out what you perceive to be the most non-violent option in the circumstances in which you are actually involved.

As one joins the lineage based upon the Pāli Canon and the teaching of the Buddha, as one joins the lineage as marked by receiving the transmission for free from the teacher who received it for free, as one turns the wheel by maintaining the centers, by helping to run courses, then one also enters into a neighborhood in which people are trying to live in an atmosphere of harmony, loving kindness and expansive good wishes. I once looked for an aphorism to capture this ethos of Vipassana and I came up with the expression, "You can never speak up too often / for the love of all things." My wife has come up with a simpler slogan. She says, "Keep on turning."

A feature of Vipassana that is worthy of an essay in itself is the complexity of psychological actions that the meditator awakens inside of him or herself. As psychotherapists, our curiosity is piqued: "How does meditation really work at the psychological level?" Meditation sounds very simple. You sit there, close your eyes, trying to neutrally observe your bodily sensations which will also make you effortlessly aware of their mental correlates, and you try not to react to whatever is happening in your mind and body, but just to observe it as it is, and you try to do this continuously over hours and days with some minor variations that you are taught, to keep the technique dynamically related to the different types of mental and physical states that you might be observing at any point in the continuum of time. The goal of all this is to become a peaceful, harmonious citizen, who is at ease with him or herself, and who brings some harmony and well being into their society and culture.

In spite of the unifocal intention and effort, multi-focal psychological catalysis is engendered by Vipassana. Many changes are being stimulated as you sit. There are multi-faceted interactions between the human psyche and the activity that we call Vipassana. In another essay I've described these psychological, developmental attributes of Vipassana in detail: "Beyond Mindfulness: Complex Psychological Development Through Vipassana Meditation." Here I will highlight just a few of the salient psychological events.

The first thing is that Vipassana is values based. It is neutral observation but it is not neutral in cultural valence. It is an education that contains a didactic root. There is an educational inculcation to value a morally preemptive lifestyle. One is taught to live by an attitude exemplified by the traditional five vows, which echo the Ten Commandments or any other practical, social, ethical way of life. The vow not to commit sexual misconduct during daily life, outside of a meditation course, means that sex should be a loving bond, which holds together an interpersonal relationship, giving continuity of affection to the partners, and providing a node of stabilizing amity within society. There is no point in embracing Vipassana if you don't share these five moral attitudes. Or if you do commence Vipassana practice with total skepticism towards the five moral vows, your meditation practice, though based on neutral observation, will not allow you to remain cynical. If you keep practicing, your meditation will rotate you on the carousel to capture the ring of these values. There is no way that you can walk the Appalachian trail while harboring a desire to become a logger like those who feel: "If you've seen one tree, you've seen 'em all." There is no way that you can walk the path of self-knowledge, realism, and appreciation, without treasuring the psychological healing and social contribution of ethical rectitude.

A second psychological development that Vipassana brings to bear is cognitive restructuring. Vipassana does not tell you what to think. It just tells you to observe. What you will observe is the adaptations and mal-adaptations of certain cognitions.

Without anyone telling you how to ride a bicycle, with no one standing behind you to yell at you, "Lean a little to the left, now quickly lean a wee bit to the right," after a few tries of trying to learn how to ride a bicycle, on your own, it becomes intuitively obvious how to ride a bicycle in the upright position by balancing this way a little bit and by balancing that way a little bit. It is an automatic education because if you don't listen to the intuitive attunement of your body to the upright position, you fall off the bicycle. Vipassana is similar to riding a bicycle. Neutral observation generates an intuitive reinforcement system for producing states of self-awareness, harmony, and peace.

The Buddha addressed cognitive restructuring through Vipassana initially by saying that one has to work hard. Meditation is not merely relaxation. Yet one cannot work hard without being relaxed, because one cannot sustain meditation without relaxation. So there is a dynamic balance, like riding a bicycle, between ardor and relinquishment of effort. The Buddha, lacking in bicycles, used the simile of a stringed instrument. We could say in modern imagery it is a guitar string. If it is tuned too tight your notes are sharp. If it is tuned too low the notes sound flat. You have to learn to tune your E, A and D strings to the proper tension. So as you sit still trying to neutrally observe your sensations, you are actually cognitively restructuring your sense of effort, to attain vigor with self-acceptance, focus with ease.

In a similar manner, many other cognitive restructurings occur. If you enter a lifestyle in which you are trying to be alert, harmonious and peaceful through twice daily meditation and through annual meditation retreats, there is no point in augmenting or maintaining anger, hatred, or avariciousness in your mind. Your meditation itself will create a feedback loop to decondition those states of mind which make you unhappy or uncomfortable with yourself, and to reinforce those states of mind which leave you feeling integrated and eased. Meditation over time will spontaneously induce a natural attrition of negativity and an unforced growth of positivity.

A third psychological, developmental contribution of Vipassana is that it is a social and communal activity. Of course one is constantly practicing on one's own in the privacy of one's own domestic nook. But meditation comes from other people. It came from the Buddha. For thousands of years it was passed on freely from person to person. Today there are hundreds of thousands of people around the world practicing Vipassana. Meditation is a journey from individual encasement to communion. The image of the stone icon of the Buddha sitting cross-legged is not an accurate representation of the real life of Vipassana. The stone icons that have become associated with the teaching of the Buddha became popular only long after his death, as his teaching was becoming lost, and have contributed to a negative stereotype. The Buddha was a physically active, long distance walker, a conversationalist and a social being, who reiterated that the Path is friendship with others on the path. No matter how experienced you think you are, you can always benefit on the trail from the feedback of other backpackers, who can clue you in to which springs are contaminated or pure, or which trail shelters harbor mice and porcupines who want to savor your gorp in the night. You walk the path alone, by the power of your own quadriceps, your own leg muscles, but those scouts who first blazed the trail, and your fellow hikers—that friendship around the campfire—even the Buddha cherished those friends-along-the-way. Vipassana has no membership roles or dues, but it brings you into contact with a human community with whom you share an ultimate concern.

A fourth psychological development of Vipassana meditation is the amount of insight into oneself that it engenders. Even one's first Vipassana course brings a transformative awareness of and integration with the contents of one's body and mind. The sensations of the body are a storehouse of mental contents and mental contents are a pictorial representation of the sensations on the body, and both express the energy which is encoded and stored in the vehicle we call "life." We are the activity of atoms, molecules, and cells; we are the ripples of physics, chemistry and biology. Body sensations are the crossroads where all of Vipassana connects. The thing we call our self is a process embedded in the psychics and chemistry of the universe. It is from deeply realizing this that one gains insight into who one really is.

So Vipassana is a practical, empirical, non-Buddhist path of self-awareness, self-development, and community participation, a meditation upon the constantly changing and transitory nature of all the phenomena in the world that one calls oneself. Every thought you have seems so important. When you are fifteen you are bent out of shape about something your pack of friends whispers, or some hint in a girl's speech. You agonize over these apparent thunderclaps. When you turn forty, you no longer remember that these things ever occurred. Someday your entire life will not be remembered by you. Everything will pass away. As one works with this perspective, one develops a sense of what is in fact of enduring value. The most enduring values are those that far exceed and transcend the confines of the individual self. We can say that there is a religious or spiritual dimension that is cultivated in Vipassana. We realize that every person is the same as every raindrop, every wolf, and every delphinium in the garden. We share with all living things the dimensions of life and death. Every living being is the child of those two ancestors. In at least those two dimensions, all beings are kin. Our personal life is very transient. There is no way to satisfy the background ill ease of death without deeply confronting impermanence and provoking a satisfactory retort to its initial nihilistic innuendo. You are set up to answer the question about what life means given the pervasiveness of impermanence. A new sense of reality about the world is experienced and internalized by all Vipassana meditators.

For this development we could use the word, "ecstasis" from which the word ecstasy is derived, and which means "ec," outside of, and "stasis" standing, standing outside your self. This is not just the observing self that one gains through psychotherapy, where one is able to observe that one is angry at one's partner, and without acting on that anger one tries to observe, understand

and augment insight into it. The ecstasies of meditation is standing outside of all of oneself entirely, standing outside of one's culture entirely, standing outside of one's historical era entirely, observing the impermanence of everything. What comes up, what one values and lives for after this vaulted standing outside, is unique to meditations that bring you to deeper experiences of the impermanence of all of your thoughts, feelings, and body. Within all of the world that you can directly contact, your own mind-body, there is no absolute reality you can hold onto. The material universe is made of different grades of sand. Vipassana can be said to steer its practitioners towards transcendence.

"Ecstasis" and "transcendence" as I am using these words do not mean an excited belief in some historically parochial ideology, some castle in the sky. Ecstasis and transcendence are loci of balance. They aren't forms of excitation. They are about standing back, watching, becoming cool and letting go. There is a great faith impregnated within the mere act of meditating. You meditate with earnestness because you have faith that there is some value to the enterprise. You have faith enough to work so hard at meditation that it carries you to new insights, new understandings, new shores.

Everyone knows that penguins are birds who have specialized in swimming at the expense of flight, but did you hear about the flock of penguins standing on an Antarctic ice flow, who looked up to see one of their friends flying over head? He yelled down to the other penguins, "We just haven't been flapping hard enough!"

Practicing Vipassana is a way of getting up. You stand outside of and transcend. You are above beliefs. You realize that all beliefs are human fantasies, yet you retain faith in the ultimate value of your life and of meditation, because it gets you high. Not excited high, not delusional high, but perceptive, highly realistic. Anything you believed in, anything you hold to be true, is merely mental content inside of one little mammal that is destined to disappear from this planet. Vipassana is a journey beyond verbal, visual, conceptual, emotional, and ideological belief. You extract yourself from old preconceptions.

The Buddha called his path "a journey beyond views." You orient by direct experiential participation, three dimensional, irreducible meditation and living. You come to understand that the path is inside you. You are the path. You are the wheel that is turning. You keep walking, beyond beliefs, views, religions, definitions, words, into a moment-by-moment reality that is opening outward. We used to say in psychiatry that it is process, not content, oriented. Reality is what is unfolding. Its ultimate nature is outside any thing. It is not containable within ideas. It cannot be grasped. You open the doors, you let go of the preconceptions, and you keep on watching and walking.

I'm still a psychiatrist and I don't want to get thrown out of my profession! So I have to mention the words, "outcome measures." Let's be as practical as clinicians can be, and talk about results. The teaching of the Buddha is definitely progress oriented. But what I hope is now very clear to you, the psychiatric treatment of anxiety and depression is not the goal and is not among the true outcome measures of Vipassana. The image of a path is about going forward, getting further away from the starting point of ignorance, and approaching a goal. The goal is *Nibbāna,* meaning, not wind, not words, not things, not ideas, not sand grasped by and slipping through your hand. Liberation. Beyond. Given this transcendent goal, what can a practical, worldly, professional affirm as a valuable result?

The path brings benefits as soon as it is activated, because starting out on the path is itself part of the goal. So a first outcome criterion is continuity, walking, treasuring and activating morality, meditation, and realization, becoming the path rather than merely complying with it, spontaneous identification and participation, going forward, starting the adventure again every day. Spontaneous means that you are not just doing it because a meditation teacher told you to do it. As you learn to observe yourself it becomes obvious to you: "These are the things that give me health and life." Meditation becomes integral with the passage of your days. Your days are intervals within which your meditation reappears and flourishes. You stop meditating because someone told you it is good for your blood pressure. You meditate because you feel: "This really helps me, essentially." You follow the organic feedback of a process-oriented life of positive volitions, and fresh takes.

We have already considered a set of psychological actions within Vipassana that are both intrinsic to it and also constitute valuable outcomes, such as self-integration, self-insight, cognitive restructuring, social affiliations, ethical positions, and embrace of change.

Another entire arena of outcome criteria is a collection of developments I call spiritual emotions. This is like a garden you plant. You cultivate aromatic and beneficent modes of being, like herbs. Meditation makes it obvious to you – "we hold these truths to be self-evident "- to inculcate, augment and relate through these emotions as much as you can, as well as you can. The spiritual emotions are those that are maximally congruent with the life of meditation, and they will eventually hover over your life like gulls above the waves. The practice of meditation attracts them, brings them home, facilitates them and is facilitated by them, in a feedback loop. A feeling of generosity…a lifestyle of generosity: you were given all of this teaching, courses, Centers, as charity. You were the welfare recipient! When it comes to meditation, you were the stray dog who was petted and given a bed. Maybe meditation Centers are not very different from animal rescue shelters. So naturally you want to feed some other strays from your old pack. A lot of the good things in life only exist when they are in transit, being given away, particularly emotions. Meditation is always taught for free for this reason, that its affectual basis includes the activity of handing it out, a Potlatch. Then there is gratitude; you are in debt to a long chain of donors and yet they are refusing to collect interest due. So you live in debt, not burdened, but grateful, appreciative, inspired by the example.

And then the feeling of reverence, not simply reverence for the symbols of a religion, just walking through the world with a receptivity for its heroes and flowers. Some of the aspects of this world are like clouds, so ethereal and impermanent, yet we are elevated by looking up at them. The world is transitory and filled with decay and death and yet you have set out on an open road that provides idealism and optimism rooted in factuality and realism. Some long-nurtured organization of events has launched you on a high road of wisdom, and you see the world as containing a path you revere, beings you revere, your own private interior gallery of founding exemplars like the Buddha or Thoreau or hummingbirds.

The Buddha taught a specific exercise to generate the feeling of loving-kindness, and the ability to do so is considered to be the premiere outcome measure of Vipassana. A feeling of loving-kindness: this is similar to when the Buddha saw a gang of kids trying to kill a cobra and he asked them, "Why are you attempting to kill someone who is only trying to be happy just like the rest of us?" Meditation is similar to music because if it stays inside you it doesn't exist. Meditation is only a rehearsal for the path, and loving-kindness is one of the cherished concertos of the concert season.

The last spiritual emotion that I have time to mention is awe. We exist within a season of an opportunity. We can awaken our consciousness and distribute love and compassion in showers the way a cottonwood tree sheds cascades of its floating white seeds.

I hope you won't wander off the path into the roadside weeds where meditation gets tangled with healing. Healing is very important, another critical human enterprise, which we all care deeply about and from which all of us earn our living. But its methods, reimbursement systems, certifications, kinds of relationships, and values differ. Its goal differs. You cannot preserve the generation-spanning beauty of the great trail if you sell pieces of it to real estate developers for malls or even for hospitals. It is inconceivable that the trail crews on the Appalachian

Trail would market their volunteerism as a new kind of mental and physical treatment, although there is little doubt that hiking is good for the mind and body.

I hope all of you will have the opportunity to walk the grand old trail, the path that crosses over the canyons of time and cultures, that leads up the mountains to vistas, but then, unlike any other trail, climbs higher than views, "the path beyond views," to a pure summit "beyond the wind."

Around the world a 2,500-year-old multi-center field trial of Vipassana meditation has been evolving, and as hundreds of thousands of people walk the path and rotate the wheel, I am an interested participant-observer, curious to see what its impact will be upon the higher mental health of the human community.

Differing Contributions of Vipassana and Mindfulness to Mental Health

Based on a talk to the Mindfulness, Meditation,
and Neuroscience Research Center
University Medical Center, Freiberg, Germany
November 19, 2007

Thank you for extending yourselves to listen to me in English. This effort to build bridges across language and culture is similar to the daily task of a psychiatrist, who attempts to understand the inner world of another person. There is, however, the joke about a psychiatrist who was approached by one of his neighbors, who exclaimed: "I admire psychiatrists so much! They make such noble efforts to comprehend and to vicariously share in the suffering of others. How can all the members of your profession have attained the admirable ability to listen so thoroughly?" To this the psychiatrist merely retorted: "Who listens?"

I want to focus you from the start on the idea that Vipassana Meditation contributes to the mental health of its practitioners, and through them, to the human community, but that Vipassana, as taught by the Buddha, and as it has been re-introduced to the world in the second half of the twentieth century by Mr. Goenka, is not intended to be a treatment for any physical or mental disorder. You cannot treat depression or anxiety with authentic Vipassana, but through the practice of it you can become a healthier person. Vipassana is less like a medical or psychiatric procedure, and more like an education, which expands your skills in living and lifts your sights regarding life's goals and purposes. Vipassana is less like medical treatment focused on a particular disease, and more like exercise aimed at optimal health. My "take home message," is that Vipassana has a multi-millennial history, like reading, like marriage, like civility and sociability, touching the complexity that makes us human. It would be a sad day when people would get married only because research has shown that the conjugal bond correlates with improved health and prolonged longevity. Similarly, I want to encourage you to think about meditation as something that touches the heart and makes one feel befriended in the deepest way. It contains so much potential beyond mere strategic convenience or medical supplementation. It is an invitation to a wider world.

I'd like to clarify why I am taking the position I am, by defining the tradition of Vipassana I represent. My teacher, Mr. Goenka, is of Indian descent, but was born in Burma and learned Vipassana from a Burmese teacher, Sayagyi U Ba Khin. Mr. Goenka eventually returned to India, his ancestral land, and began conducting Vipassana courses around 1970, in both Hindi and in English. Over the past thirty-five years his courses, now taught by his appointed Assistant Teachers and Teachers, have spread around the globe. There are scores of Centers throughout the world dedicated to this dispensation of Vipassana. Germany has a center, and other Centers in countries near you include Belgium, Switzerland, France, Sweden, and Italy. When I made my first trip to India to study preventive medicine in 1970, the word "Vipassana" was essentially unknown, even there. Today, there are Centers from Mongolia to Chile, from New Zealand to British Columbia. A remarkable teacher has received an international welcome.

There are two authenticating signatures of this tradition. First, it is transmitted from teacher to pupil. A person doesn't practice it and then proclaim, "I am a Vipassana teacher!" A student may, after some time, be requested to take up the responsibility of becoming a Vipassana teacher. So there is a transmission, person-to-person, and the lineage preserves itself in an authenticated form.

The second hallmark of the tradition is that it refers itself back to the Pāli literature. Pāli is an ancient Indian language, an offshoot of Sanskrit, in which the Buddha's teachings were preserved. The Vipassana tradition, which I am going to be talking about this evening, is preserved in the Pāli language and the practice is consistent with the words of the Buddha. It is possible to still practice meditation just as the Buddha did.

The word "Vipassana" was invented by the Buddha. It means to see realistically or to see clearly. So Vipassana is observation, seeing things as they are. You can immediately get the idea that this requires no religion or philosophy. Mr. Goenka is not a Buddhist. I have not been converted to Buddhism. I don't call myself a Buddhist. The essence of the practice is to live a way of life that is realistic, practical, in keeping with the laws of nature, healthy for oneself and making one a productive and contributory citizen to the lives of others. Meditation creates a feedback loop to give you information about how your way of living actually impacts your mind. It creates a mirror of well-being. So Vipassana is not just something you do when you are sitting still. It's like biofeedback, but in this case, bio-psycho-spiritual feedback. Your meditation creates a circle, in which you are communicated back to, from your meditation, about your way of life. A simpler image would be that it is a compass pointing out the true coordinates of existence. To gain this directive power, it needs to be learned in an adequately rigorous way.

Vipassana is taught in a ten-day residential retreat. That's very different from being able to learn something in an evening seminar, or in a weekend class. It requires enough of a commitment to leave home and immerse yourself in new and unknown territory. The course is also taught in Noble Silence, meaning that for nine of the ten days you can't talk. Of course you can always talk to your teacher, or to the managers of the pragmatic details of the course, but Noble Silence means that your intention is to be silent in your mind, silent inside yourself, silent between you and others, silent in word and silent in deed: no gestures, no telephones, no computers, no email, no reading, no writing, no keeping notes. Silence. Occasionally there are people who think of this as unsettling or frightening. There are also people who hear about this and immediately decide to attend, just to have ten days of silence. There is a story about a person who bought a brand new very high tech cell phone that does everything: text messages, emails, photographs. He is talking on his cell phone while walking down the streets of New York City and suddenly he says: "Stop! Stop! Wait a minute. I think I just took a photograph of my ear." At the very least, a ten-day Vipassana course is a vacation from the frenzy of the modern world.

It's interesting that at a slightly different angle, but in kinship with the growth of Vipassana, there is a growth in "Mindfulness," to which your research center is devoted. "Mindfulness" is not the same as Vipassana, but it shares the effort to recover concentration in a culture of distraction and mental invasion. Many people feel they live in "1984," where something is systematically worming into the privacy of our minds. Ten days of silence is exactly the opposite. It is not intended as an imposition of silence onto you. It is meant to lift burdens off your shoulders.

Another feature of the course is that it is surrounded by a moat of moral vows. Vipassana is realistic observation; however, it is not exactly a scientific stance towards the world because it is encircled by ethical commitments. The historian of religions, Mircea Eliade, said that modern civilizations are based upon the conjunction of the numinous and the ethical. The "numinous" means the things you consider holy, sacred, or awe-inspiring. Primitive religions have ritual at their core. Rituals are generally intended to get favors from some higher power, the implication being that the higher power can be bribed or bought. In opposition to ritual, the conjunction of the numinous and the ethical means that those two become one, your ethics and your sense of the holy. It is ethics that are holy, that constitute the ladder by which we can climb up to the higher reaches of the psyche, from which we can look down and gain perspective. So there's an emphasis before the course begins on taking vows. When I took my first course in India in 1974, and I came upon these vows, I felt uncomfortable. I felt someone was trying to impose their rules onto me. I felt slightly insulted. Was someone condescending towards me that I had to take a vow not to kill? I worried that I had stumbled onto some puritanical religious teaching. Later on I came to realize that the vows are a practical doorway. The ethical vows are not to kill, not to steal, not to lie, not to use intoxicants, and for the ten days, to live in celibacy. Of course Vipassana as a path does not require people to live in celibacy, but for the ten days one is completely alone, completely oneself, completely private, completely in silence with no physical or emotional relationship with anybody. The goal of this is not religious. The goal is practical. It's like preparing to fly a jet, and you are positioning the plane at the right angle on the runway to take off in the correct direction. The goal of Vipassana is to make these ethical attitudes an intrinsic part of all your waking moments so that you go forward in life always headed in the right direction.

You are also asked to take a vow to practice meditation exactly as you are taught. That seems pretty obvious, but during ten days, day and night, many people are tempted to go back to some prayer that they once learned or to some other meditation technique that they once knew. So you are asked to follow the instructions without deviation. Give it a fair trial. After you have done so and you don't like it, of course you can throw it away; but if you give it a fair trial there is every reason to expect that you will like it much more if you diligently follow the directions.

The first three days you are taught an introductory form of meditation in which you meditate on your breath going in and out. It's probably the simplest direction you have ever gotten in your life. You're just sitting there observing your breath going in and out. This sounds like it should be easy, very pleasant, very peaceful. But those of you who have never tried it, I guarantee, it will drive you nuts. And those of you who have tried it are already nuts. It's very hard. We have all learned to relax our nervous systems by overloading them. We create relaxation through exhaustion. Typically we work, or maybe you are at home as a mother taking care of children, and your day is busy. Then you say, "I'm tired. I feel stressed. I want to relax. I think I'll put on the DVD; I think I'll read a book; I'll listen to some music. In order to relax I will now stimulate my nervous system through the auditory; I will now stimulate my nervous system through the visual; I will now stimulate my nervous system though the audiovisual." We relax by creating increased stimulation. In our daily life in the modern world we never loosen the string of our nervous system. We are either busy or we are relaxing by making ourselves busier. So when you get the direction, "Just observe the breath going in and out," your mind and body begin to crave something else. "This is boring! I want something else; I want something interesting; I want sound, lights, action!" The capacity to merely relax and observe has been lost to most of us.

Now a word or two about the use of the word, "mindfulness." "Mindfulness" is used differently in the Vipassana tradition than it has come to be used in the Western world today. "Mindfulness" is a neologism, a new word, an invented word. "Mindfulness" was not a part of the American English vocabulary thirty years ago. The practice of Anapana, watching your breath, which I have just been describing, is an exercise in learning how to control your mind. It is not meditation *per se,* but an exercise in developing the proper type of concentration that is most useful for meditation. It is not what is meant as mindfulness according to the teaching of the Buddha. When you are watching your breath moving in and out, you are developing mastery of the mind, the ability to direct your mind to a subtle and relaxing focus, and to have your mind obey your intention. Almost any person who is functional in this modern world feels: "I *am* in control of my mind, or I am mostly in control of my mind." Actually we are not in control of our minds at all. If you give your mind a large dramatic task, your mind will obey you.

For example if you say, "Read this book," your mind will read the book. "Walk to the store." You will walk to the store and your mind will guide you. But if you say to your mind, "Watch your breath and don't do anything else," your mind will say, "No, I'm not going to do that." And you say, "I'm the boss. I'm telling you to watch the breath." But don't expect your mind to obey, because it won't!

Back home in Massachusetts we have a very wonderful dog who we adopted from an animal shelter. Everyone asks us what breed he is and I just say, "Yes." He's every breed, you could say, breed enriched. He is very funny looking, very cute with glossy golden fur, and very affectionate, but he has got some hound dog in him and he is totally his own boss. He is not one of these dogs who is a pathological pleaser, who always does what human beings tell him to do. He does what he wants to do, an independent thinker and a free citizen of the world, who likes to let you know that he has a choice about this obedience thing. If you say, "Come here," he runs over to the far side of the yard. If you throw a ball for him to fetch, he won't move, implying that he does not want to be patronized as some sort of inferior animal known as a dog. If you don't pick up the ball, he'll pick it up in his jaws and growl at you and rub it in front of you, to entice you into action. His behavior also expresses our human minds when we try to do a subtle, nuanced, quiet task. It is its own boss. Our mind rebels and returns to seeking stimulation, and excitation, which are the common ground, the things we have learned how to do. When you start Anapana, concentration on the breath, you will find out you ain't nothing but a hound dog.

Every day for the first three days you get slightly varied directions on the same practice. You are taught very carefully; you are not left to wander on your own. You are given exact and specific guidance, working on the capacity to observe and concentrate and to be the boss over your own puppy that you call your mind. It is true that in the beginning it does drive you nuts. But in three days you begin to make significant progress. There are periods where you can't control your mind at all. Just storms of daydreams come up. Then you gain a little more capacity, and have moments of exquisite simplicity of focus and calm. Now this concentration is not mindfulness as defined by this Vipassana tradition. It is concentration. Mindfulness as we understand it is the next stage.

For the next seven days you practice Vipassana; that is, mental awareness of all the sensations in the entire body. You are taught very gradually and slowly. Day by day the directions change. You start in a gradual way, how to move your mind through your entire body, such that your mind and body become integrated. The task of your mind is to be aware of your body, and your body enters into full communication with your mind. There is no longer a separation between mind and body. Typically we live as if we are hovering in our head somewhere looking down upon our body. But in Vipassana you gain the capability of dwelling inside your body. It is the awareness of the constantly changing sensations of one's own embodied life that the Buddha called, mindfulness. At times you can experience them all at the same time. At other times you can experience them sequentially.

Now the focus of Vipassana is sensations of the body throughout the body as continuously as possible; *sensations of the body, throughout the body, as continuously as possible.* That's the actual definition of Vipassana that the Buddha used. Having established this mindfulness, the goal, the meaning of Vipassana, is to be completely at peace. The whole teaching of Vipassana, although it takes ten days of instructions, lectures, and effort, yet actually it is so simple, it is almost embarrassing. What you are learning to do is to observe yourself, to do nothing else, and to be calm and peaceful. You are not superficially pretending to be calm when you are really just distracted and avoiding the agitation within you. You are not aware and caught in turmoil. You are fully aware, and equanimous. Couldn't be easier. Except that when you practice it, you recognize that you are not easily calm and peaceful, because there are a lot of things that you don't like, and there are lots of things that you wish were different, that you don't have.

The human being is constantly torn from calm and peace of simple existence by two things; wanting what you don't have, or disliking what you have.

For example, you are sitting still, you are trying to be peaceful, you're meditating, you are feeling sensations throughout your body, there are many different sensations, more than you have ever been aware of because you are now meditating systematically, with perseverance, turning your attention only to the sensations of your body, and there you are, the world should be as good as it gets. You have no problems. They feed you home made meals; you've got ten days of silence; you do not have to go to work. If you've got teenagers, you don't know whether they are driving your car or not; what could be better? And the first thing you think is, "I don't like this. My back hurts." And the second thing you think is. "I'm hungry. When is lunch?" I don't like what I have. I have a sensation in my back and I don't like it. But what I don't have, I do want: I don't have lunch. I want lunch. Your mind is constantly seeking to find dissatisfaction because the way we have been conditioned to live is to find something new, to stimulate our nervous system, and create some new pattern, vigilance or entertainment. We have lost the ability to simply sit there and be calm and peaceful. So Vipassana is a training or an education in how to observe and not to react, how to come to terms with, and be peaceful with, all the sensations within the matrix of "you."

Now the very important word that I keep using repeatedly is "sensations." Let's look at why this was the focus of meditation given to us by the Buddha. If you are just observing your body in a global way, you say, "I am aware of my body," but in fact there are many things going on in your body that you are not actually aware of. So you are actually not being calm and peaceful with your body. You are imagining you are calm because you are only half aware of what is going on. Unconsciously, you are reacting inside. Full awareness reminds me of looking for birds in the forest. If any of you are birders you know that if you stroll through the woods, you will hardly see a few birds. If you go with an expert, the level of observation changes. Somewhere up to the left there is a Rose Breasted Grosbeak. In the high branches of an oak is a Tennessee Warbler. The more a person attunes themselves to picking up subtle signals, the more they will observe. Vipassana teaches you to pick up the subtle sensations, the subtle signals of the whole body, throughout the body, systematically and perseveringly. This means initially that there is a lot more to be dissatisfied with. You are aware of more things, so you have more to complain about! "I hadn't previously given much attention to my back; now I know it hurts." "I didn't know I was hungry. Boy, now I really recognize those hunger feelings. I feel hungrier." It also means in the long term, there's more that you have learned to be calm and peaceful with. So as more new sensations enter your consciousness, once the course is over, once you have returned home, you've developed a way to be calm and peaceful with a great diversity of signals from life. You have learned to be at one with yourself at a deep level. You have practiced systematic equanimity.

Part of Vipassana, which used to be difficult to explain, has become easier to explain: the mind and the body are the same thing. When I started psychiatry, we were still trapped in the Western hemisphere. Things like Vipassana hadn't come over. There were no institutes like this, where the difference between East and West has been erased. I am told that Buddhist monks come here and scientists study them so you don't differentiate what is East and West. But when I started my profession, Cartesian dualism was still the dominant way of understanding: we have a mind linked to a soul independent from our body. Now that illusion has been set aside. One of the dramatic ways we learned about the identity of the mind and body, which influenced me greatly as a developing psychiatrist, was the Vietnam War. I started my psychiatric training in the United States in 1971. There were many young men returning from Vietnam who were seriously traumatized. The psychotherapies that were tried with these traumatized veterans were partly successful but inadequately so. A traumatized person is usually completely rational, non-psychotic. Say a war veteran returns home to a pleasant, peaceful town like Amherst, Massachusetts, where I live—it's similar to Freiberg, except that we do not have one-thousand-year-old castles!—but otherwise it is safe, clean, bucolic. Still, the veteran cannot relax. He lives in terror. You say to him, "How can you be terrified? It is totally safe here." He replies to you, "I know it is safe. But I cannot feel safe." If you inquire about how these former soldiers feel, they experience ongoing in their body the sensations of combat. It is the sensations that endure.

It is not true that the mind is in the brain. It is not true that memory is in the brain. Mind and memory are coded in the whole body. Trauma is stored in the library of the body. Today, no matter what school of therapy you are from, we treat trauma with the understanding that a person is traumatized throughout their whole body and their memory of trauma is in their body. This is tragically true in women who have been raped. Obviously their memory is in their body. It's also true of soldiers. It is also true of people who have been through large-scale traumas like 9/11 or flooding or the wars in Yugoslavia.

The mind, as a synthesizing and organizing receptor, notes information that is stored throughout the entire organism. And the entire organism serves as a memory bank from which the brain receives and reorganizes information. When you are meditating on all the sensations of your body, gradually, not all at once, as your meditation becomes deeper, the entire memory of your life becomes available to you.

In spite of how hard you have to work at a Vipassana ten-day course, the Centers in Europe and elsewhere are almost always overbooked. The most attractive magnet about Vipassana is the sense of integration with yourself. You become who you have been. You become truly yourself. Most people are not traumatized, and contain castles full of pleasant and unpleasant memories. As you work on awareness of sensations only, you are not trying to think, you are not trying to remember . . . but memories, dreams, visions, flood your mind. They are the other side of the coin of sensation. Sensation is the physical representation of mental life. Mental life is the pictorial and verbal representation of sensations. When you get in touch with many sensations, subtle sensations, the intricate, varying sensations throughout the body, your whole mental life is open to you and you become a person who we say is mindful and self aware.

Let's return again to the word, "mindfulness." Of course no one owns this word. It can be used any way its owner chooses. But mindfulness as described by Vipassana practice begins specifically with awareness of sensations in their constant variation and change. The body is constantly changing. It is full of sensations, which are changing. The mental life that interacts with and perceives them is also changing. Every human being is an aggregate of changing things. In science we say we consist of atoms and molecules and cells and tissues. We are organized into these large-scale beings like mammals, but actually we consist of all these little particulates, which themselves are probabilities of the location of energy densities, and we live for a period as the temporary organization of these aggregates, and then we dissipate. Every human being is vibrating and changing, as do the energy fields and waves and particles of our atomic substructure. As you meditate on the sensations of the body, you get in touch with the fact that there is nothing solid, nothing constant, everything inside of you is changing. This awareness of change is the definition that the Buddha gave of mindfulness.

Mindfulness, as defined by the Buddha, means awareness of incessant change, of arising and vanishing, inside of your own body, which is the ultimate reality of your own life.

Each of us blindly experiences ourselves to be an individual self-propelled little deity. But in fact we are products of physics, chemistry, biology. In the American West we have dry storms (I don't know if you have anything like it) where the dust swirls in a whirlwind, and you see a standing "person of dust"—sometimes colorfully called a "devil-dog"—held aloft by the wind. When the wind dies down, the devil-dog disappears. That is like us. Vipassana is awareness of the change, this insubstantial quality of all human life. Mindfulness is the quality of awareness coupled to the object of awareness that enables this realization of change, impermanence, and insubstantiality. Mindfulness has this specific denotation to a meditator.

Mindfulness is not the same thing as the "mindfulness" which consists of focused attention on external objects and tasks. A criminal breaking into a first floor window is focused and intensely concentrated, with both precise yet scanning attention. Aware of his slightest gesture, alert to every flutter or whisper around him, he is nevertheless not practicing mindfulness. A sniper on a rooftop in a war-torn city is intensely activated and keenly attentive, but not mindful. These people cannot progress on the path of Vipassana meditation as taught by the Buddha.

The word "mindfulness," as taught by the Buddha and as intended in Vipassana practice, is based on moral intention, introspective self-awareness, and insight into nature's laws as embodied in our own body-mind.

Now I've described three of the most important features of Vipassana. The first, as you meditate on sensations, unintentionally but inevitably, your mental life rises up in front of you and you are actually meditating on mind and body integrated. The second is that you become aware that your entire body/mind is changing second by second, in fact, millisecond by millisecond, and has no enduring essence. The third is that you are cultivating inner peace as you observe without reacting.

Well. What's next? Your initial foray into meditation is quite self absorbed, filled with yourself. One of the features of the human body is that it is built to feel pain. If you didn't feel pain, you wouldn't be aware of the necessity of extracting yourself from certain noxious situations. So our body is designed to feel pain, and that's a problem because every day, more or less, we feel pain, but we avoid it by running away from it. When you are meditating and you've decided, "Well, okay, I'm going to sit here and observe everything that comes up," one of the things that comes up is pain. So you do need to learn how to observe pain and other unpleasant physical sensations, like hunger, sleepiness and restlessness.

But also, even more difficult, is that pleasant sensations come up. When you are able to meditate on your whole body and you are feeling subtle sensations vibrating everywhere, it feels exceptionally pleasant. It creates a bliss beyond anything you experience in daily life. In some meditation traditions these states are cultivated and misconstrued as the goal of the practice. But if you are meditating to become a balanced person, then craving after temporary states of rapture is just another transient and illusory craving. The goal of meditation is calm and peace, and here you are getting carried away either by unhappiness, like, "I don't want this pain," or pleasure: "Oh, this is so blissful, I think I will quit my job and run away and just live in a monastery and meditate!" Either of those are intoxications that strike the meditator as he or she is first becoming aware of this vast reservoir of thought and feeling and memory and daydream and wish and fear, craving and aversion, that is stored in the body.

Vipassana meditation is learning to surf the waves of craving and aversion, without drowning in them. But that is not all. Another thing begins to happen. You begin to experience moments, increasing moments, of clearing from this narcissistic drama with which we fill ourselves. "My life is transient. Really, life has no meaning if it is just about a little animal that scurries around sniffing for food and other brief 'fixes'."

My friends here in Freiberg took me to the center of the old city today. I don't know if those of you who are born amidst these scenes can freshly apprehend how remarkable it is to an American. The oldest buildings where I live are two hundred and fifty years old. On this patch of the planet, here, one thousand years of beauty has been stored up in the buildings and arts, like the stained glass windows in the cathedral. I was transported by the colors of light streaming through the red and golden glass, and then we left the cathedral and we were walking through the streets, where there was so much shopping going on, and I thought: I've discovered the religion of Freiberg, a new religion to replace the old one: it is shopping. Of course, I come from the country that invented the shopping mall, where you hardly even have to walk in order to purchase a plethora of imports. You poor people here actually have to go outdoors and get cold hands as you wander from store to store! Is that all? I'm not against shopping, but is that all? When we were walking down the street in Valladolid, Spain, just a couple of days ago, some kid had scrawled with chalk on a wall in Spanish, "Work. Consume. Die." Is he on target with the factual critique? Has he accurately pinned down the insect specimen of our lives?

Whether you are religious, whether you are an atheist, whether you are a cynic, whether you are an idealist, there is no value to a life that isn't filled with something more than your own pleasure and pain. We call it love, we call it community, we call it compassion. As the narcissistic drama fades in meditation, and as I say, it doesn't totally fade away even if you have been meditating for thirty years, but it fades, and what rises up is the other side of the human condition. It's true that we are only animals. It is true that we are only passing clouds of electrons and other sandy, ephemeral stuff. The Buddha's teaching is not just about the tangible world. Our practice is to observe realistically. We are not throwing in any god. We are not throwing in any Buddhism that you have to stir around to flavor the pot. But there is something beyond the tangible world. We are not going to name it or label it, because as soon as we do, people will start fighting over what name we have given it, and how big we believe it to be, and what books "It" is alleged to have authored. If we say "God," someone will say there is no God. If we say, "It is not God," someone will say there is a God and we are sinners for denying it. No name facilitates our true experience and understanding as we descend into the deeper layers of meditation. We directly encounter the realization that there is something more to life. So, if I were to scrawl Vipassana graffiti on a wall, it would be: "Work, consume and before you die, meditate to find something more."

And that something more is always going to be a gift, something you give. That is why authentic Vipassana is taught for free. No one gets paid. Even tonight there was a question as to whether we take any money. We don't even accept an honorarium. Our centers are run entirely for free. People take a course entirely for free. If someone feels like it, they leave a donation. You will never be asked, though of course most students do leave a donation so that the wheel of free courses can continue to rotate. Obviously we feel people should work; money isn't bad; we aren't a socialist-anarchistic movement! Vipassana is for free because it is a transmission of a spirit. Those who have learned it are eager to give it away, because, if you keep meditating, something will rise up in you that will be a clearer, stronger consciousness, ennobling your life. This "something" may be labeled differently by different people, but meditation raises the blinds and the sun shines in. Something more than pleasure and pain will enter your life and you will become wealthy in its largesse and will be in possession of gifts. Maybe Vipassana is no more than spiritual holiday shopping! Something to give away, like a treasure from a fairy tale: the more of it you distribute, the more it fills your shopping cart.

Vipassana can be said to operate in two directions: it reduces craving and aversion, and it augments realism, generosity, and the value of life.

Now the health benefits that come out of this dual action are various. One thing is that body-mind integration does reduce some stress and psychosomatic syndromes. There's a funny story that our teacher tells. Mr. Goenka was born in Burma though he was a Hindu, and Indian. Under the British those countries were blurred; Indians wandered into Burma and were living there. Mr. Goenka was having migraines, and someone told him migraines are psychosomatic headaches and if he took a Vipassana course he might get rid of them. So he went to his Burmese teacher, met him for the first time and said that he wanted to get rid of headaches and would like to take this course. "Can I take it even though I am a Hindu?" His teacher replied that being a

Hindu was no problem; the course is not Buddhism. But if you want to get rid of headaches, there is a big problem: you are not welcome. The goal of the teaching is not to treat headaches. There are other treatments for headaches. Use those. The goal of the course is to walk the path to that "something else," that love and compassion, that generosity, that is beyond the mere materiality of the world. In fact the ten-day Vipassana course cured Mr. Goenka's headaches, but only after he had given up the goal of curing them! So Vipassana leads to improved body-mind integration, and a certain amount of psychosomatic illness will fall away, but we do not advocate people taking this to cure psychosomatic illness. I had a professor once who was explaining what was wrong with nuclear power. He said nuclear power is used to run generators that rotate from the pressure of the steam that is generated. You heat the system to thousands of degrees to boil water at one hundred degrees Centigrade. It's an extravagant waste of energy.

Vipassana is not a supplemental medical therapy. It is the ancient wisdom trail leading to the kingdom of what all people, religious or atheist, Eastern or Western, cherish.

Now going on to mental illness, the same thing applies. We don't advocate Vipassana for the treatment of mental illness because the course is hard. There is a tremendous amount of nurturance, and affectionate support, but the fact is that when you are meditating, you are alone inside your own mind. If there is somebody who cannot follow directions, for example a person who easily becomes delusional, then how are they going to meditate? They'll forget the directions and just end up spinning in their delusions. If someone is very overwhelmed with anxiety, if they have panic attacks, they are not at all delusional, but how can they learn to meditate in the middle of a panic attack? It's unfair to ask someone to do that. So we do not advocate Vipassana as a treatment for specific psychiatric syndromes. Vipassana should augment self-knowledge, self-integration and social commitment. Those are its mental health benefits

Social commitment: how did it ever come about that the Buddha is portrayed in those cross-legged statues, sitting still, not giving a damn about anybody else? If you actually read the ancient texts you realize that the Buddha never stopped walking around. He was very physically active. A portrait of him sitting still is very inaccurate. He traversed large swathes of Northern India on foot, multiple times. He talked all the time. If he actually talked as much as the preserved texts attributed to him, he talked almost non-stop. He was a very social person, not an anti-social person, explaining with repeated commitment how to improve life. When I went to medical school I just sat in a library and studied books. No one ever portrayed doctors as people who sit still in a library for the rest of their lives reading. The Buddha may well have sat still cross legged under a tree, both when he was on the path to *Nibbāna,* and afterward, for part of each day, when he was an active teacher. He was never a statue, never a solipsist, any more than a studious doctor is.

In meditation you do sit still, close your eyes, you turn off the world and you turn on mindfulness of the arising and passing of all the sensations of the body with the awareness of the impermanence of yourself. But then you get up and live, taking the heart of what you found and putting it back into society in any way that is appropriate to you and to your skills. That's good for anyone's mental health. Anybody who can take a ten-day Vipassana course will get some mental health benefits that are quite dramatic and wonderful although not in the sequence you might want. You can't say, "I'm a depressed person, I want to take a Vipassana course and in ten days cure my depression." We don't know in what sequence which particular problems will be dissolved, and which particular benefits will light up in your life. Some people feel that one of the first benefits is increased organization. "Because I focus twice a day, I am a more organized person." Other people say some weight is lifted as a particular conflict yields to the practice of equanimity. Other people feel: "There was some traumatic life memory I had, of my mother's death from cancer, and during the ten days, as I was working on a certain sensation over here, I began to have a memory of her last days again and again for two days in a row; I was caught in this memory; but I did Vipassana correctly; I didn't try to roll in the memory; I kept trying to meditate on the sensation... and, by God, the emotional drama of those events has gone." Other people find forgiveness replacing anger, or direction leading out of confusion. The technique of working with the body layer of the mental life liberates you from many problems that you are carrying with you, but the particulars of sequence and substance are as unique as the individual life story.

This multifaceted, individuated, cross-cultural conjunction of the numinous and the ethical, this thought-provoking, emotionally stirring pursuit of wisdom to live by, this mix of morality and insight into individuality and community, this probe of meaning and purpose beyond the materiality of existence, should not be reduced to concentration exercises, nor to mechanical scanning of the body. Studying whether meditators can perform mechanical tasks better, like improved monkeys, is not really scientific investigation of meditation or of mindfulness at all. Such studies reduce meditation to concentration, and measure the least common denominator of focused mental activity. No one devotes themselves to meditation in order to improve their scores on a pencil and paper test designed by a Harvard assistant professor who needs the data to get tenure.

The best way to measure meditation is by its outflow into the human community, its effusion of virtues, its reduction of egocentrism ... or its failure to do so. Is our sweet Noble Silence really fruitful in the dark night of warfare, environmental degradation, over-population, and poverty? Do rigid dogmas and their self-righteous war cries still hold sway, or is a tenacious, ameliorating realism getting heard? Is commercialization of leisure still spreading agitation and obesity through the economically advanced but spiritually impoverished nations? Is there even a small alternative lifestyle, based on meditation, equanimity, and service, threading its way from people to people, sewing together gentle, wise, and hopeful friends?

The Buddha said that teaching Vipassana always requires metaphorical understanding as well as literal understanding, because metaphor evokes important aspects of our capacity to understand. The two key metaphors of Vipassana are the path and the wheel.

You walk the path. Vipassana is not very meaningful if you do it once. It is interesting. For people who are psychologically minded, it is fascinating. The path, however, leads beyond merely interesting experience, to lifelong development as a fully human transmitter of awakened and harmonious life.

The Buddha said that when he started his teaching he turned the wheel. If you rotate a wheel, friction will stop it. Someone else has to come and rotate the wheel for it to keep spinning. We are the generation now alive. If we don't keep spinning it, the wheel will stop. So as a meditator you gain a pleasant responsibility.

The Buddha described his path as the path beyond all views. That something more that you get out of Vipassana—it is nameless because it lies beyond ideation. Vipassana friendships sew together Marxists and Catholics and Hindus and doctors and salesmen and housewives and military veterans and pacifists. The Path leads forward wherever you start, and it goes beyond all views. You are walking up the mountain and in an ordinary life you get to the top to see a beautiful view. In Vipassana you walk to the top of the mountain and you keep on ascending beyond all views.

Clarification of Mindfulness
in the Context of Vipassana Meditation

For a person who chooses to practice Vipassana meditation in the tradition of S. N. Goenka and teachers of his lineage, mindfulness is a central component of an integrated, well-rounded practice. Mindfulness is not utilized as an isolated entity, but as a guiding feature of a full meditation that leads to wisdom and growth on the path to liberation.

It is as if an outdoorsman were setting up his tent in the White Mountains of New Hampshire. He must carefully loop every corner to a stake, and snugly rope every flap to a firmly embedded tent peg. The tent stands aloft and secure as an integrated whole. If one corner is loose, or one flap pendulous, the wind will play upon it, rattle and loosen it, and in the middle of the night the tent will begin to shimmy, flap wildly, and eventually collapse. The tent is useful if the outdoorsman understands and properly balances the interconnections of its parts. No single feature, no matter how tightly strung, can hold aloft a tent. Similarly, mindfulness strengthens a meditator who properly understands its connections to the other features of Vipassana, and who keeps them in balance.

It is as if an outdoorswoman were hiking the Appalachian Trail from Georgia to Maine. Only if she understands the nature of the trail—its mud, rocks, streams, and steep inclines—will she select the sturdy, water-repellent boots that the hike calls for. To avoid the blisters or frozen feet that drive so many hikers off the trail, she needs insight into what the long trek entails. Similarly, mindfulness without insight will not outfit a meditator for the long journey of wisdom.

Mindfulness has a specific meaning within the context of Vipassana meditation. It means awareness and understanding of the arising and passing nature of every sensation within us. This particular understanding of mindfulness will interconnect properly with the other practices that constitute the Path, like one part of a well-constructed tent, and will also allow long distance, lifelong progress, like well-chosen hiking boots.

Mindfulness as an aspect of Vipassana is different from focused attention on external objects or tasks. A criminal breaking into a first floor window is focused and intensely concentrated, highly aware of every slightest movement and gesture, but he is not practicing mindfulness. A sniper on a rooftop in a war torn city is alert, aware, intensely activated and keenly attentive, but his activity will not lead him forward on the path taught by the Buddha. Their attention lacks moral intention, self-awareness, and insight into nature's fundamental laws.

Mindfulness for progress in Vipassana means attention directed inward towards sensations with the goal of understanding impermanence and cultivating an ethical and loving life. Mindful apprehension of sensations elevates into consciousness the basis of the previously unconsciously developed false sense of self. Our bodies and minds are constantly interacting. The mind is incessantly receiving myriad sensations from the body. When this interaction is unconscious, the result is the common human delusion that we inhabit, or consist of, an enduring entity, a self. Many of the sensations, which underlie this misperception, are subtle, and not easily available to our consciousness awareness without practice.

Mindfulness as the active engine of Vipassana is the effort to concentrate, to re-focus, to persevere, in establishing and re-establishing full awareness by the mind of bodily sensations, gross and subtle, with which it is constantly interacting, and through this conscious, mindful awareness, to realize that every sensation and the entire self is impermanent.

The realization of impermanence that derives from right mindfulness reveals that the self is a static concept imposed upon a dynamic rising and passing, vibrating and changing field of atoms and molecules. Through this practice, meditators can experience their own body and mind as part of the shifting flow of the material of the universe. Realizing there is no essence, no self in this on-flowing process, the meditator naturally cultivates detachment from the fantasy of self. As detachment arises, craving for and clinging to the self diminishes. As right mindfulness on the sensation-based direct experience of impermanence and no-self grows, it is spontaneously accompanied by release from craving and from aversion for particular sensations. As objectivity replaces craving and aversion, a sense of freedom and harmony takes their place. The increasingly peaceful and accepting meditator naturally cultivates fewer negatives states, and finds himself generating love, compassion, and a desire to serve and spread this helpful liberation.

Mindfulness is the compass on the path from ignorance and reactivity towards the north pole of equanimity, generosity, and freedom. The compass itself is incomplete without guidance, effort, commitment, realization, insight, companions, practice, and experience—the whole path.

Vipassana Meditation, Mental Health, and Well-Being

Gregorio Marañon Hospital,
Obstetrical Department
Madrid, November 16, 2007

I've never given a talk in an obstetrical hospital before. I hope everyone has not come here tonight to see me give birth!

I'm going to focus on Vipassana, which is one particular kind of meditation, and I'm going to clarify its unique contribution to mental health. I will not be saying that Vipassana cures psychiatric illness, which is a claim sometimes put forward by some other types of meditation. What I will be saying to you tonight has an ironic quality: the more a person practices Vipassana meditation to get health benefits, the fewer health benefits they will get. The more a person practices Vipassana meditation for its total contribution to their life, the more health benefits they will get. Vipassana is not a treatment. It is a way of life to enhance well-being at many levels in many ways. Only by focusing on its essence can one obtain its peripheral additions.

There is a famous story in our Vipassana tradition of our Teacher, Mr. Goenka, going to his Teacher and saying he wanted to learn Vipassana to cure his headaches. He was refused admission to the course! The goal of Vipassana meditation is not to cure headaches. He had to agree to take Vipassana for its spiritual core, for its total contribution to his life. He agreed to do so with initial reluctance, but he did finally enter the course in the manner intended. After ten days, Mr. Goenka ended up with his headaches being cured. Because he surrendered the narrow healthcare goal and embraced the larger humanistic goal, he benefited at the level of health but also at many more levels, which ultimately enabled him to become a world-wide teacher who has had a beneficial impact on the lives of hundreds of thousands of people, from Chile to Mongolia, from Canada to New Zealand.

Because Vipassana has such wide effects upon the total person, I want to tell you a story illustrating the difference between a focus on health, and a focus on the complex human dimensions of life. There was a young doctor who had recently completed his medical training. He was a very modern fellow, well informed about preventive medicine. He was committed to the idea, which most of us have also embraced, that diet and exercise can be very helpful in preventing illness. But he was also a post-modern man who unfortunately had lost touch with some of the higher aspirations and deeper dimensions contained in human life. He was a typical contemporary mechanist and materialist. Well, as the story goes, in the town where this young doctor was working in the emergency room, there was an elderly couple. The elderly man was known to have a weak heart. One day he had crushing chest pain and his wife wisely called the ambulance. The ambulance arrived, and immediately raced the patient off to the emergency department. The wife followed behind the ambulance in her car. Of course she could not keep up with the ambulance and arrived about ten minutes after it had. She was met at the door by our young doctor, who gave her terrible news. He said, "Your husband has died of a heart attack." Naturally, the woman was stunned with grief and began to weep. But our young doctor, a good-hearted soul, tried to soothe her by saying, "Don't worry, don't cry—in the ten minutes between your husband's arrival at the hospital and his actual death, I was able to give him one last, modern, up-to-date lecture on the importance of diet and exercise."

There is more to life than life.

Vipassana is a meditation Path, a meditation tradition that teaches us there is more to life than life. A human being wants more than merely healthy survival, although we want survival also. Vipassana is something that enhances existence by redirecting our sights higher than mere survival itself, towards the inspirational, universal realizations, which direct, ennoble, and bond our mere duration to higher meanings and purposes.

Vipassana is an ancient meditation tradition that is aimed at reorienting our lives.

The word "Vipassana" was used by the Buddha to describe the meditation that he himself practiced. But Vipassana is not the same thing as Buddhism. My teacher, Mr. Goenka, is not a Buddhist. I have never called myself a Buddhist. Instead, Vipassana is a practice that fits best with the empirical traditions, like medicine and science. Its basis is realistic observation of oneself.

Let's look at these two important words. Realistic means nothing added, nothing subtracted, no religion, no philosophy, just the facts. Observation means you yourself determine what the facts are, based on what you yourself experience while meditating.

Our great American poet, Robert Frost, wrote:

> "Anything more than the truth would have seemed
> too weak . . .
> The fact is the sweetest dream that labor knows."

In Vipassana we work hard to get the facts. By observing ourselves only, we open a window on the bigger picture.

One of the unique features of Vipassana as taught by Mr. Goenka, is that a student has to go away for ten full days in order to learn this technique. Frequently, I'm invited to speak at a conference, particularly a medical conference, where different kinds of meditation are taught. The lecturers are asked to give a demonstration of the kind of meditation they are talking about, usually a ten-minute demonstration. Imagine my embarrassment when I have to say, "This meditation can only be demonstrated during a ten-day long period." Other people seem to teach meditation in minutes. Why does it take ten days just to learn to close your eyes and meditate? Vipassana has as its goal the ability to change your heart and mind. It puts you on a path, a way of life that is healthy for body, mind, and spirit. From the healthy way of life, both physical and mental health benefits may flow. But the goal is not any specific physical health or mental health "fix", but a path of life itself.

Now let's look at what the teaching of a ten-day course is like. The course consists of nine days of Noble Silence. Noble Silence means you are free to talk to the Teacher or to the course manager if you have some problem, but otherwise your attempt is to be silent. Silence means not merely silence in speech, but silence of mind. You are asked to refrain from reading, writing, using a telephone, using a computer, watching television, or even taking notes. The meaning of this is not to deprive you, but to free you up, to focus you and to diminish annoyances and distractions. Next, you are asked to take vows not to kill, steal, lie, use intoxicants, or to commit sexual misconduct. The goal of these vows is not to acquiesce to repressive religion, but simply to orient the jet to fly at the right angle when it takes off from the tarmac. The vows put you in the right frame of mind for learning a practice of observation and harmony. You are also to practice the teaching exactly as it's given to you, without adding anything, without subtracting anything, giving it a fair trial. The technique has been used for 2500 years, so the request is: "Try it as it is: don't change it at all, and give it a chance to reveal its value."

The course is explained in a clear, detailed, precise manner. There's nothing mystical, vague, or difficult to understand. Every day the directions change and a new feature is added, so the description I will be giving this evening will be somewhat simplified and generalized.

For the first three days you are asked to focus simply upon your breath going in and out. Remember our description of Vipassana as realistic observation. There is nothing other than ordinary facts of life. So the introductory form of meditation is observation of the simplest manifestation of life: breath goes in and out.

You have taken a vow to practice exactly as you're taught; in spite of your vow, you find out that you are completely incapable of following the directions! Your mind starts wandering into the past, your mind starts leaping forward into the future, your mind desires to do absolutely anything except stay with the breath.

A number of years ago we adopted a puppy from an animal shelter. He was a very wild little puppy and he reminded me of my own mind when I tried to meditate on the breath. Whatever you told him to do, he would just run around the yard for fun. Sitting still is so boring. Human beings are nice but they are so dull. He could see no purpose in sitting and obeying when there are sticks and balls to chase, not to mention cats.

Why is the mind so incapable of following a direction like, "observe the breath"? I have good concentration; I studied for about a million years to get through school. Why can't I meditate on my breath? All through life, we calm ourselves down by adding new stimulation to our nervous system. When I want to relax, I read a book, I watch a movie, I turn on music. I add stimulation to my eyes, to my ears, to my intellect. In ordinary life, we never relax through the removal of stimulation unless we are trying to fall asleep. The first three days of the ten-day course are the first time most people have ever just tried to sit still with reality. Just being with bare reality as it is, observing it, adding nothing, taking nothing away. You are not trying to entertain, stimulate, or amuse your senses. Once you begin to adjust to this calmness and simplicity, it becomes quite wonderful. In spite of the initial difficulty, at the end of these first three days most people feel they've opened a door to a new world. The self is satisfied to be within the self.

For the next seven days of the Vipassana course you are taught to expand your attention throughout your entire body. The teaching is stepwise; each day you expand your attention in a new way, so I'm just giving a general description. The focus, as you now understand, is realistic observation of the sensations of the body. The body is a collection of atoms and molecules organized into cells and tissues. Throughout this organism there are thousands of sensations all the time. Usually, we are aware of sensations in our body, but only very obvious ones; hunger, back pain, the pressure of our bodies upon the chair. Actually there are thousands, and I mean thousands, of sensations happening every minute all the time. Meditation is the skill of learning to keep your attention focused upon these sensations as they rise, fall, and change, without reacting to or interfering with them. A living organism is a dynamic, vibrating field of atoms and molecules. Change is continuous, incessant. The ever-occurring changes at the level of atoms and molecules produces a ceaseless field of sensations. The meditator learns to observe them neutrally, without commenting, just observing.

Now you may be thinking, "So what!? There are a lot of interesting things to do in life; why should I just sit there observing all these body sensations changing?" This brings us back to the irony of meditation. Vipassana is the entry into a new psychological world in which, instead of expecting or demanding, we observe without comment. Instead of wrestling with reality, we befriend it. Because our observation is calm and peaceful, we become deeply aware of new levels of reality, at the same time that we are cultivating inner peace. We are following the suggestion of the English poet, William Wordsworth: "…among least things, an undersense of the greatest…" Instead of trying to manipulate life, to create health or anything else, we have taken a time period out of our routines to learn a new skill: the art of integration, the attitude of harmony, the skill of neutral observation.

As we make a continuous attempt to observe only body sensations, in fact we observe our minds as well. Mind and body are two sides of a coin. Every time the mind changes, the body changes. Every time the body changes, the mind changes. The two are completely interlocked. First, let's takes a few very simple examples. If I don't eat for a day, I will begin to get strong hunger sensations. As I get hunger sensation, my mind will start thinking about food, food, food. By changing my body, I've changed my mind. Supposing I begin thinking of somebody I really hate; I can't stand what they did to me; I'd love to give them a piece of my mind. My body will become tense, my neck muscles will tighten. By changing my thoughts, I've changed my body.

Those examples, of course, are very crude stereotypes. During the 20th century, modern psychiatry abandoned mind-body dualism. Today all the mental health professionals would agree that if you change someone's mind, you change their body, and if you change someone's body, you change their mind. This compound picture, replacing the previous mind-body dualism, was forced on Western psychological sciences during the era at the end of the Vietnam War. We had many traumatized veterans coming back to the USA who didn't seem able to recover from their trauma. They were completely rational people, yet they behaved irrationally. They would walk around in fear in a completely safe place like the small town where I lived and practiced psychiatry. You could ask these war heroes, "Why are you afraid; you are back in the USA; it's completely safe." They would say, "I know that it's safe, I simply cannot get rid of the fear". That's because fear is not just in the mind, fear is also in the body. Technically, we say that these traumatized veterans continue to emit the neurotransmitters of fear. Their nervous systems, their endocrine systems, are conditioned to continuously put out chemicals of fear. The external stimulus is gone, but the physiological habituation continues.

Fortunately, we are not all traumatized, but every one of us recognizes that what I just said is true of us also. We all have conditioned fears that are carried with us even to places where they are obviously not rational. If you have the good fortune to take a meditation course, at some point in the ten days, while you are just sitting quietly and peacefully, an old fear will come up on your mind. But meditation will give you a new skill. Instead of rolling in the thoughts of fear, you will turn your attention to the body. You will not try to get rid of the fear. Instead, you will just try to observe, "What happens in my body during this state of mind?" At the obvious level there will be things like a racing heart and dry mouth, but at the subtle level there are many sensations that will be unique to each person. If you try to stop your fear it makes you more fearful because you realize that you can't stop your fear. That's why we call it fear! It makes you feel out of control. You feel you cannot control yourself. But if you learn to observe your fear in its intricate pattern of sensation on the body, it will arise for some time and stay for some time, and then pass away. Instead of repressing it, struggling with it, trying to gain control over it, or observe its mental contents (which are fear-inducing and will make you increasingly fearful), you have practiced the meditative skill of observing your fear at the level of the sensations that it evokes in your own body. Over time, this fear will become less strong and over more time it may well disappear. Of course we can't guarantee how quickly this will happen, or if for every person it will happen every time. But the principle is absolutely true for all people all the time. The principle is that by turning attention away from your thoughts back to your body, you become familiar with yourself in a new, calming, objective, rational, helpful way.

But it is not just fear that is stored in the body. Peace and calm are also stored in the body. Wisdom is stored in the body. Wisdom is not an idea. Smart and intelligent ideas are very good things but are not wisdom. Wisdom is already in the body, but it is not so easy to contact it when you are constantly distracted by external stimulation. If you learn to sit calmly, and to observe your sensations, wisdom will spontaneously rise up in your mind and in your life. What do I mean by wisdom? A great feeling of blessing to be alive, an appreciation for all that you've been given, a sense of companionship with all other living beings, a desire to help others. Whether you are a Marxist revolutionary, a

Catholic, a Buddhist, an atheist, you will recognize this as wisdom. When you get rid of the noise and distraction, you will find that you already possessed wisdom to a certain degree. Wisdom is the cognitive component of the emotions of peace and love. As you practice meditation, wisdom can grow stronger and become more familiar to you. You will learn to contact it more easily. I describe Vipassana as being a search engine in which you can more easily locate the websites of wisdom without getting so many false search results.

So now we can see two ironies of Vipassana. The first is that it gives its best results to those who can surrender, before they start, the desire to fulfill a specific demand. The second irony is that the ability to observe without trying to manipulate or change the object of observation actually ends up transforming what we are observing. By accepting ourselves exactly as we are, we stop being who we were. The Buddha described this process with a natural metaphor.

Suppose there is a stagnant pool in a country like India, which has a monsoon climate. It has not rained for months. The water is black, fetid, thick with impurities. Now the monsoon has arrived. No god has sent the rain; it is strictly a product of impersonal natural laws. The rains commence with a single drop. The raindrop hits the surface of the stagnant pool, and with it comes a minute amount of oxygen and light. Another raindrop . . . another tiny aliquot of oxygen and light. Now the monsoon clouds burst, and thousands of drops beat down into the previously stagnant pool, not only bringing oxygen and light, but stirring and churning the water so that bottom water mingles with the surface. As the rains soak their way in, the entire pool, from top to bottom, becomes purified by light and air, becomes sweet smelling and sweet tasting. In just this manner, the mind of the meditator penetrates the entire body with awareness and equanimity, and a healthy new life is born in the body of the old life. Purification does not have to be added as a third process. The addition of light and oxygen, awareness and peace, itself brings transformation to mind and body.

After a person completes the ten-day Vipassana course, they have the opportunity to begin a new life. This new life is called "walking the path." That means that every day you have the opportunity to meditate in the morning and evening. The meditation acts like a compass. You keep getting lost and turning away from wisdom but the compass shows you the correct way back. Of course we all do get lost during our busy days, but it's a wonderful thing to have this compass to guide you. When you meditate and develop calm, peace and wisdom, when you meditate and let go of fear, anger, hate, you are doing a systematic treatment to your body and changing its neurotransmitters. Before, you systematically shot your body full of neurotransmitters of fear or hate fifty times a day. Now you shoot up that drug of fear and hate many fewer times a day. Before, you used to take a healthy herb of wisdom just in a small pinch every day. Now you take this healthy herb of wisdom in a pungent brew twice a day. Systematic, long-term meditation changes the biochemical basis of your body. Some neurotransmitters are systematically reduced, other neurotransmitters are systematically increased.

As you become more familiar with your body, you also make new choices. Those choices are different for everybody, but every continuous meditator will change habits in their diet or exercise, or their way of life. You also change your interpersonal habits. If you relate to people with less fear and hate and more love and compassion, you're changing your own biochemistry. If you become less hostile and less irritable, the people around you also get less hostility and irritability fed into them. It's possible that you even change the biochemistry of the people around you. There are studies that show that having a pet dog will increase your grades in school. There's a study showing a pet dog decreases your blood pressure and your heart rate. Susan and I both come from families where there's a lot of high blood pressure. Her father and all of his relatives had high blood pressure. My mother and all of her relatives had high blood pressure. Neither Susan nor I have high blood pressure despite our age.

I don't know if that's because we have a dog or because we meditate.

You notice I'm hitting on two sides of the same point. Meditation is not a medical treatment for anything. If you have a mental health problem, or physical health problem, it's wise to seek the help of a good professional. Meditation is taught in large groups and in an educational atmosphere. All students are treated the same. Meditation is taught entirely for free; it is not a professional service. At the same time, I've shown you the logic of how meditation changes the biochemistry of your body, the choices that you'll make, and possibly even the biochemistry and the choices of people around you. I started by saying meditation helps by helping a person establish a healthy lifestyle, not by curing diseases. Everything I've described to you so far can be summarized by the metaphor of "Walking the Path." There's another metaphor that describes meditation: "Turning the Wheel."

Meditation has always been taught for free. It was never a commodity or service to be sold. Meditation is spread from person to person in a community of friends. It's a complex learning process that takes many days to learn and when you get it for free and learn to meditate, you have to help others learn it for free, or the wheel will stop turning. Therefore, there's another very important benefit of meditation: meditation places you in a community of like-minded people. There's no membership card, there's no dues. There isn't even an exact name for this disbursed group since we don't call ourselves Buddhists or anything else. But when you really enjoy meditation and are delighted by the benefits it's given to you, you feel eager to turn the wheel. Turning the wheel is an act of generosity. It's only fair because you got the technique from someone else who was turning the wheel.

But actually all human beings are selfish. I'm selfish. I turn the wheel because it helps me. There's a great philosophical discussion as to whether altruism really exists. I know quite well that I help people partly out of compassion and partly out of selfishness. There's nothing that feels better than helping people find something that will delight them, that will make them healthier, that will give them better mental and physical health while they walk the path. When we turn the wheel, that is, when we help others, that also changes our biochemistry. In studies of both healthy aging or studies of people who've been traumatized, the single most important factor in health is having a network of people who care about you and who you care about. Not only that, the modern world is breaking down most of those interpersonal networks. But I'm myself the kind of person who doesn't like clutching and intrusive groups. Meditation and the part of meditation referred to as "Turning the Wheel" helps you be part of people where all are trying to become a little better. You help yourself while helping others. You don't even know which comes first. The Buddha said, "Friendship is not an important part of the path. Friendship is the most important part of the path".

One final metaphor that can be used to understand Vipassana is the metaphor of *Nibbāna*. *Nibbāna* is a Pāli word, which is translated into English as, "no wind" or "no motion." But *Nibbāna* can't really be translated as a single word or phrase. It can be understood by approaching it from two directions. *Nibbāna* means a mind that is completely free of all negativity; free of anger, hatred, ill will, doubt or fear. Another direction for approaching *Nibbāna* is to think of it as whatever lies beyond the material and mental world. *Nibbāna* is the goal of the Buddha's teaching. Metaphorically you can understand it as that point where a pure mind punches through the veil of physical things to the unborn, unchanging, undying, Beyond. So *Nibbāna*, which is the goal of the path, can be understood as if it were the prow of ship, the point where two guiding things join together. Juan Mascaro, a famous translator of the Pāli texts into English, who was himself a Spaniard, likened *Nibbāna* to the pole star.

Whether *Nibbāna* is understood conceptually, or whether *Nibbāna* is not understood conceptually, is not as important as walking under the guidance of the pole star. Whether you arrive or not, on route you will be cultivating the purity of mind, compassion and love: and you will simultaneously be immersing yourself in an ancient and ongoing worldwide communion of like-minded friends who not only walk the path, but who are living manifestations of the path itself. You become a disciple of the pole star of *Nibbāna*. You feel gratitude to be following a star. You receive and convey loving-kindness, which is the fragrance that arises from a purified mind. These, not the healing of diseases, are the health benefits of Vipassana.

Questions and Answers

Gregorio Marañon Hospital
Obstetrical Department
Madrid, November 16, 2007

Q: When someone is meditating and they are losing their concentration, is that time valuable?

A: Yes it is. Even though you feel that your mind is completely lost and wandering, if even for a second you are on target, that second is worthwhile. At first this seems counter-intuitive. Why is that one second on target more powerful than the wasted minutes of wandering? Aren't the lost minutes much more powerful, and therefore the loss column bigger than the gains? Let's look at an example: an infection has taken over your body. Your doctor will give you an antibiotic. It will just be a tiny pill or a tiny injection of fluid, much smaller than the sixty or seventy or so kilograms of your body weight, but that small dose will clear your body of bacteria. A small rectifying moment is more powerful than days of disease. Even seconds of meditation will give you a certain amount of clarity. Your mere effort also is fruitful. You are trying to wake up into clarity, even if it remains elusive. A few drops of precipitant and the cloudy bucket of water clears. Of course, if you keep practicing, those seconds will grow and increase.

Q: I have attended a number of courses. Why does Mr. Goenka pay so much attention to the anatomical and physiological sensations, and not so much to the sensations of negative emotional states such as fear?

A: Let's see. We'll have to go over this carefully because certainly you should pay attention to the sensations of negative emotional states like fear. I think you may have misunderstood. You are supposed to pay attention to all sensations. Remember that fear itself is an abstraction, so that what you can actually observe are the bodily sensations that accompany fear. When you are learning the step-by-step process you are encouraged to keep moving so that you learn to observe your whole body. At that stage, you observe sensations, but then move on to new areas of the body. But after those step-by-step practices, you should pay attention to every sensation in your body...every sensation including those connected to fear and other negativities. By observing the sensations that accompany the negativities, you can stop rolling in them, and begin to let go of them.

Q: In a world filled with all sorts of social groups, what criteria can we use to define ourselves as a group that is non-sectarian, and to differentiate ourselves from other groups that define themselves by what they are? How can we identify ourselves as a group in a non-sectarian manner?

A: I think that meditators become a loosely defined group by functioning together to create meditation courses for others, and by taking meditation courses ourselves. It is our activity, and not our identity, or brand name, that defines us. I have a friend who is a Catholic nun. I have a friend who is a Marxist activist. They both have been Vipassana meditators who have sat and served from time to time. They both have helped rotate the wheel. Possibly what you are implying is that, even though we do have a sense of community with our co-meditators, we have a porous boundary. We are friends together, but we are not interested in making an exclusive identity, in creating in-groups and out-groups, in becoming an institution or feeling separate. Being a meditator does not eliminate our other participations.

We don't have badges or even dues. But we do look forward to group sittings. Meditating with other people in silence can be remarkably communicative. To some extent, that is our group. But our extended group includes all living things. We don't want to separate ourselves from all beings. We are a group opening outward rather than a group enclosed within.

Q: Can Vipassana meditation be delicate for people in states of crisis?

A: Anything can be delicate for a person in crisis, and at our Centers we do inquire into people's health and well-being before they take a course. We try to make an intelligent discernment whether it is appropriate for them to take the course at this point in time, or whether it would be wiser to wait. Some crises are moments of opportunity; but it is unwise to launch into one's first Vipassana course when one is fragile or unstable.

Q: Is there a problem with Reiki and Vipassana? What is the problem?

A: Vipassana is a practice that is based upon neutral observation. Reiki is said to be based upon trying to move your sensations, trying to make them flow. So there is an intrinsically different, antithetical intention. Vipassana means observing without any attempt to interfere. That is the difference.

Q: Some meditation schools use mantras. Vipassana does not. Are these different paths compatible? Do they conflict with each other?

A: Good question. There are two reasons why Vipassana doesn't use mantras. The first is that mantras can be seen by potential meditation students as sectarian, and Vipassana is non-sectarian. So the name of a god or a deity or any culturally sensitive word is not used. But the deeper reason is the one that I spent more time discussing during this evening's talk, which is: working with sensations of the body brings us into deep contact with our bodies, our minds, our feelings, and the laws of nature as they manifest within us. We do not fix our attention on one sound. We come in contact with many layers of reality within the world of ourselves.

Q: Can you comment from the scientific point of view what are the effects on meditation of using mantras?

A: I can't specifically comment. My home is in Vipassana, and I don't practice or study mantra meditation. I know that there are many positive benefits that have been found. The two meditations are friendly activities, sharing a world of people who want to live in peace and harmony. There is no point in stirring up competition or antagonism between the two. But obviously you can't do two meditations at the same time. It is like marriage. Pick the right person for you without condemning everyone else's partner. But let's avoid meditation-bigamy! All of human development requires stable, focused, committed long-term growth. Any one person can grow in meditation only by developing one practice.

Q: Is wisdom something that comes out of meditation or is it just something one has to learn intellectually?

A: Wisdom is a word with many uses. In Vipassana we take it to mean a life of love and compassion and joy and peace. My American hero, Thoreau, said that his attempt was to so love wisdom as to live by its dictates, a life of simplicity, independence, magnanimity and trust; to solve the problems of life not only theoretically, but practically. In these uses of the word 'wisdom', it does not refer to information or ideas as much as to the emotional tone of life, the quality of life, and the skills to bring them to fruition. After all, we can have ideals, but every day life is hard and challenges us. Intellectually, one can understand wisdom and set sail in its direction. To cross the ocean, to keep sailing every day in the direction you believe is wisdom, meditation is the ideal vessel.

Q: Mr. Goenka says that sensations have to do with craving and aversion. Do specific sensations have specific meanings? Does itching convey different meanings or is this over-intellectualizing?

A: There are many causes for sensations. They are not all caused by craving and aversion. The classic example is if you turn up the heat in this room, we will all feel heat. If we turn down the heat in this room, we will all feel cold. So temperature of the environment can induce sensations. Sensations can also be caused by our personal life history. If you have chronic tension you may get neck spasm. If you had an auto accident ten years ago, you may still feel back pain. It is not the sensations themselves but our reactions to them that are of most importance. Generally, sensations provoke our reaction of either desire or fear, craving or aversion. The issue for a meditator is not: what sensations am I having and what are their various meanings? The issue for a meditator is: Can I become aware of myself, my life, and all that it entails, at the level of constantly changing body sensations, and can I dwell in peace, harmony and calm observation of them?

Q: Dr. Fleischman! First of all I would like to thank you for being here and talking about meditation. I'm somebody who has practiced Vipassana and has also practiced yoga and *pranayama* for some time, and I would like to make an affirmation and I would like you to tell me whether it is correct or not. I think all these other practices—yoga, *pranayama*, Reiki, which was mentioned before—are not limited to observation. They do attempt to change sensations. But this doesn't mean that we should stop doing all of these other techniques, because as a matter of fact they benefit people even if they are attempting to change rather than to observe sensations. I think we should be conscious that they are techniques which can't be done while we are practicing Vipassana, and that we should never try to modify the Vipassana technique by incorporating new things into, nor subtracting anything from, the technique. But during other times, for example, during my day, I could be practicing yoga or Reiki to help myself or others.

A: I've done yoga my whole life so there is no conflict vis-à-vis a routine physical health activity and Vipassana. But if a person really wants to gain the benefits of meditation at the depth that I have described in this talk, and there are even more depths that we didn't have time to discuss, one has to enter into deeper relations with the practice. That depth does require a cessation of other activities that are similar to but different from Vipassana. An analogy is that if you are a teenage boy in the West it is perfectly reasonable, and as a matter of fact it is advised, that you go out with different girls. But when you reach a certain stage of life, you may want to have an ongoing relationship, and you can't keep going out with your teenage harem. You neither condemn all the other females on the planet, nor boast about your steady partner, but you make a choice and grow within the context of deepened love and mutuality.

There is a similar maturation in the life of a meditator. Focus on the meditation you find best for you, and marry it, make it your partner, the centerpiece of your life. Then you will spontaneously put aside other meditations, or other meditation-like activities, which use mental volition for systematic interior focus. One does not have to condemn or create a competition with these other meditations. But any other activity, which entrains your mental volition repeatedly, will become an obstacle to walking the path of Vipassana to its real goals. Yoga can be practiced as a merely physical health exercise without mental training. But constantly attempting to change your body sensations will cultivate a habit, which will contradict your cultivation of an observational stance in Vipassana. Vipassana means to see things as they really are. No matter how much you manipulate yourself, the laws of nature remain. Vipassana means observing reality within yourself at that depth.

Karma and Chaos Revisited

University of Vienna
November 24, 2007

Thank you for listening to me in English. I am going to talk about "Karma and Chaos" with a particular focus on how these concepts apply to the life of someone who meditates regularly. I am not going to discuss "Karma and Chaos" as pure ideas, but as tools for a practical application. The application is to live a life of meditation.

Karma is a very helpful way of understanding reality, particularly if you are a meditator, and chaos theory is a useful introduction to the way a Western educated person can more clearly understand karma. My practical focus, only talking about these ideas as they apply specifically to Vipassana meditation, reminds me of a story about two dogs. One dog was from Paris. He was very rebellious, very individualistic, didn't believe he should take orders from anyone, and he said to his other canine friend, "I've been studying human beings and I think they are terrible. They cause wars; they're warming up the climate of the entire planet; they're leading to an extinction of all our fellow mammals. I think we should stop obeying them. We should stop wagging our tails at them." His friend, the second dog, was from Chicago, so he was also a rugged individualist, but he had too much of the American pragmatic attitude to be as anarchistic as a Parisian. So he replied: "I agree with everything you said. I can't disprove any of it. However you should remember that human beings are the ones who know how to open a refrigerator door."

The Buddha emphasized the importance of karma. He used the word *kamma*, which is a Pāli word, but I am using the word karma, which is a word that has become part of the English vocabulary. For the Buddha, karma was not a philosophical add-on. He emphasized karma as intrinsic to his teaching. Today there is a lot of meditation being taught in Western Europe and in the Americas that is based upon an experience of immediacy, being aware of things in the moment, which is an excellent and important feature of meditation, but it is not the whole story. There are also meditations in which students are encouraged to accept beliefs that are called, "Buddhism." Buddhism, said in this way, is an "ism," a systematic form of thought. So to say "Buddhism" implies a cognitive, philosophical system based upon the teaching of the Buddha, which is waiting for a student's acceptance or rejection. But what I am going to steer you towards is the teaching of the Buddha, which happened before Buddhism was invented. Buddhism was invented hundreds of years after the Buddha died. The Buddha's teaching was based upon direct experience of reality via Vipassana meditation. He wanted people not to have an idea or a philosophy, but to meditate, dip into an experience, and based upon their own experience, to live a good life. When I say the Buddha emphasized karma, that means he hoped it would rise out of the Vipassana experience as an intrinsically meditative insight.

One of the Buddha's chief disciples, Sariputta, came to the Buddha's teaching in the following way. He was walking down the street when he saw one of the Buddha's first five disciples, Bhikkhu Assaji. Sariputta, who was a very cautious and skeptical intellectual, said to Assaji, "I hear you are following a great teacher. What does he teach?" Assaji said, "He only teaches one thing. If there is some effect in this world, there must have been a cause. If you don't like the effect, take away the cause. That is the entire teaching of my teacher." Of course if a person is looking to reduce or eliminate their suffering, then Assaji's words are very powerful. If there is an effect called suffering, then there is a cause for suffering. If you don't like the effect, get rid of the cause. This bare-bones definition of the Buddha's teaching, as given by Assaji to Sariputta, was the expression of karma. The explanation was so simple, logical, and unimpeachable that Sariputta immediately began to follow the Buddha's teaching, to practice Vipassana meditation, and became the chief historical disciple, and was eventually proclaimed pre-eminent in wisdom, second only to the Buddha himself, in instructing people in the Buddha's methodology..

The word, "*Buddha*" was used in the time of the Buddha, and subsequently, but actually the Buddha usually referred to himself by a different term, the *Tathāgata*. It is a term that is variously interpreted. The word literally means, "thus come" and "thus gone," which is really quite ambiguous. What does it mean? In its more poetic form, it means the Buddha was an emergence, a manifestation, of universal truth. He spoke universal truth and then he merged back into the universal truth, so he came thus out of the universe, and he went thus back into it. But the Buddha gave a very practical, less poetic definition of what it means to be the *Tathāgata*. It means, "Someone who sees cause and effect everywhere." That's exactly the meaning that Assaji gave to his teaching. The teaching of the Buddha is not just to be-here-now, not just to be mindful in the moment. He gave absolute, definitional importance to causal thinking, to the awareness of sequence and consequence.

In the days when I was seeking a kind of meditation for myself, and as someone immersed in the scientific tradition, I couldn't imagine following something that didn't have logical, rational, causal explanation for how meditation worked. So in the old days and in the modern days this emphasis on causality, on the universe as being logically understandable, has been inviting.

Karma is a way of looking at things that is a part of right understanding. It is also the essence of right action because it is both our intentions and the actions into which intentions become translated, which become part of our karma.

But there is a difficulty with karma, and this is one of the reasons why it is intriguing for me to look at chaos theory and see whether it could be helpful to our contemporary, Western minds. The difficulty with karma is that it's not always obvious where our karma is coming from or to what karma really refers. The word can be casually bandied about as a post-hoc description of events, to endow them with the aura of understanding, under circumstances in which the term has been dug up to obscure insight. It becomes a "buzz-word" that hides truths more than explaining them.

One feature of the *Tathāgata's* pointing towards the term "karma," is that it's a concept or tool that can be applied only to oneself. The Buddha said that we cannot use this word or this idea of karma when we look at other people. When you hear it colloquially, in common speech, divorced from the actual teaching of the Buddha, someone will say, "Well… that man had a heart attack and he was a smoker…you know it was just his karma." To this, the Buddha might well reply, "Well no, you are not using that word correctly, because you are applying it to someone else as an implicit judgment, that subtly devalues him and makes you seem superior." Or someone might have generous intentions and say, "That guy worked very hard, he trained and trained. That's why he won the Olympic marathon. What great karma!" To which the Buddha might still reply, "No, it's incorrect. Only a *Tathāgata*, only one who sees cause and effect everywhere and understands it perfectly can apply it to someone else." So when we are talking about karma we are exclusively talking about a tool to help us understand ourselves. Each tool has its proper realm. There's a story about a person who heard that laptop computers have become the most important tool of modern society, and so he borrowed his friend's laptop computer to hammer in new shingles on his roof. Each tool can be well applied only in its proper sphere.

Karma is something we apply when we look at ourselves through the lens of Vipassana meditation as part of a causal, sequential, logical, lawful universe.

But it is not always intuitively obvious that "karma" is true!

People will say, "How did I get this disease? I never did anything to create this disease. Why can't I get rid of it? It's unfair! My friends, who are no better people than I am, don't have any illness this bad. I just don't deserve this."

Or people will say, "I've been meditating quite seriously. I've taken many ten-day Vipassana courses. I've practiced meditation twice a day, every day, and I still have this certain problem that I came with. I have been working hard to get rid of this problem and after five years I still have the problem. If karma worked, I would be rid of this. I don't think karma is a valid concept."

We see things that we don't like about ourselves, or we see things that we have worked to get rid of in ourselves, or we see things that we don't understand in our life situation, of which we feel only a victim. We don't feel we caused all or even most of our life. So how can the Buddha's statements—that as you get wiser you see cause and effect everywhere, that understanding cause and effect is the key feature of the teaching of the Buddha—how can we integrate this with our personal experience, which often doesn't connect causality to our circumstances?

Just as karma can be properly applied only by oneself to oneself, similarly, karma makes sense within the context of meditation. To understand your life through karma, you need to witness your life through Vipassana.

If you are going to meditate, it appears that you will be relinquishing some degree of control over your life. For example, if you are a student and you meditate, well, you are not studying. If you are a parent and you meditate, well, for that hour, you are not taking care of your child. If you are a worker and you meditate, you are not earning your keep for that hour. So meditation requires some confidence that what you are doing is valuable, that what you are doing will contribute directly to your life, that it will, in fact, improve your karma. To gain confidence, one needs to clearly comprehend the contributions to life that meditation does and does not make. Both Vipassana and karma need to be understood in the context of each other, and both need to be apprehended correctly.

What defines Vipassana? It's not the same as all meditations; it's not just any meditation. It's a specific meditation defined by a number of features. First, Vipassana is taught for free. The Buddha gave it away for free. If we think of the Buddha, a *Tathāgata*, as someone that the universe manifests, through whom the universe gains a voice and explains what the universe is about—well there will not be a fee charged for the universe's teaching. The universe is not saving for retirement, nor is it currency-hedging Euros against the dollar. Vipassana is part of universal life. It comes along with reality as the practice of experiencing reality within one's own body and mind. Vipassana exists as part of what can't be claimed and sold as someone's possession.

The second feature of Vipassana: it's logical, rational, based upon causality and karma. This is what we will be exploring for the rest of our time together today.

The third feature of Vipassana: it's always taught as part of a moral or ethical worldview. To learn Vipassana, it is necessary to adopt an ethical attitude. That's different from the many meditations that stand exempt from moral necessity. Vipassana always commences with moral vows, not to kill, not to steal, not to lie, etc. It is caring, care taking, and not merely expediency or narcissism.

And finally, Vipassana meditation focuses on the sensations of the body, and more specifically, Vipassana focuses attention continuously, as continuously as possible, on the sensations of the body, so that one can observe the change, the constant change, incessant change, that goes on in the body. The transition from birth to death is accompanied by constant change, which is perceivable by each individual as he or she examines themselves during meditation. That change is happening all the time, every millisecond, continuously. So Vipassana as taught by the Buddha is part of an ethical way of life in which you observe your sensations, your bodily life, constantly changing, changing, changing. There is not a fixed or artificial focus outside of yourself. Instead the focus is to look inside of yourself and to see reality, and reality means the incessant transformations of which life consists. Understanding this change means understanding the causal sequence as events rise up and pass away. Each sensation is caused by the previous moment.

A human being is a sequentially causal phenomenon. When you meditate on sensations of your body you immediately perceive two laws of the universe. One law is that everything is changing. The second law is that change follows serial and harnessed sequence. One event causes the next event. Each event every moment flows into another one in the same manner as a river flows.

But when we look at our life as a whole, sometimes it's difficult to see the causality. We don't see what caused our good fortune. And we don't see what caused our problems. Sometimes it's easy to see; sometimes it is hard to see. So let's look, as scientists, and see whether we can give a meaning to karma that is consistent with our modern scientific thinking. We don't want to fall prey to blind belief where we say that everything that happens to me is karma but I have no idea why. I don't know why I got this disease. I don't know why I have a good education or a bad education. I don't know why I was born in the United States or Europe. And just to say that it is karma, well that's just belief. So let's apply scientific thought to this problem and see what we come up with.

Early scientific thinking was based on linear cause and effect. The classic description of linear cause and effect is if you play what we call "pool" in the United States (I think you call it billiards) you take a cue stick, you hit one ball, and that ball hits another ball. It's possible to predict exactly what the second ball will do. If you took physics in high school or college, you learned that the momentum of the first ball and the angle with which it strikes the second ball, gives you an exact and perfect prediction of what the second ball will do. That's Newtonian physics. I had to study that in high school and college and that's the model that doesn't seem to apply at all to our experience of our lives! If I got a disease, where did it come from? What was its clear and immediate antecedent? Who struck a ball that gave me this disease? Or what did I do to get this disease? If I was born in the United States, how did that happen? Who caused it? Did I cause it? How could I have caused that? The simple science by which post-Renaissance Europe built the modern world, the science that led to machinery, the science that led to the first stages of medical treatments that were non-superstitious, that science was a wonderful gift to all of us—that science doesn't help us understand karma. In fact, it appears to invalidate karma.

If we look at the sciences that try to understand more complex phenomena, I think we will understand karma better. I don't know if any of you are good at playing pool but if you are terrible at it, I remember times when I would take the cue, strike the ball and it would just bounce off the table. And when it careens off the table it bounces around like crazy. And there is no physics teacher in the world who can predict and explain how it bounces in the way it does. We need to understand that crazy bouncing ball which is more like the way human life is actually subjectively experienced.

There is a form of equations that describe the universe in a mechanical linear way. Those are the equations we generally study in mathematics. An equation is a law or a statement and the statement creates a line, a picture, a graph, and that line gives you the ability to predict into the future based upon the original statement. But there are some equations that create very irregular shapes—non-linear equations. They were difficult to study before computers because the calculations become very wild. You can take the same equations and out of them will come very variable patterns. To study so much variation, you need a computer that can run equations out many iterations, many repetitions, faster than a human being can calculate.

The first field of science to which computerized, non-linear, complex equations was applied was meteorology, weather. It is very important for us to predict weather; it determines our commerce and our health; and yet weather appears quite chaotic. It does not follow a fixed pattern, particularly here in this country of valleys and mountains, and also where I live in the Northeastern United States, where weather can be extremely variable. It can be 20 degrees one day in winter, and -20 degrees two days later, or it can snow, rain and be sunny on the same day. As scientists began to study weather, they realized predicting it through linear mathematics is totally useless. It's like karma. Causality is difficult to discern. But predicting weather patterns through non-linear equations graphed by computers gives us some ability to predict the future, and that is why typically today, when we listen to a weather report, it is somewhat accurate for one, or two, or three days ahead. It gets decreasingly accurate as we look further into the future, but we have some ability to predict the weather.

One of the key scientists who helped to predict weather more accurately was a meteorologist named Lorenz, who studied non-linear differential equations for forecasting the weather, using graphing computers. This goes back to about fifty years ago. One of the first things Lorenz discovered was that although weather varies greatly, it does not vary totally. There's variation, but there is order within a particular zone. For example, the sun radiates millions of degrees of heat. Conversely many of the planets, like Neptune and Pluto, are absolutely cold. But earth varies only about 100 degrees, an incredible phenomenon. Our weather very rarely gets above 40° or 45°C anywhere, ever. And it very rarely gets below minus 40°C anywhere, ever. Why? Why doesn't it occasionally get up to 50° or 60° or 80°, which of course would end all of our lives? The difference between 45° Celsius, and 80° Celsius, is after all a small difference considering the large differences that are theoretically possible, and which other planets have. How does the planet manage to stay within a zone of 100°C? This is one of the great mysteries, connected to atmospheric gases, distance from the sun, tilt of the planetary axis, and other variables. I hope it is not going to change! It looks like it might! Lorenz discovered that all of the variation in weather that New England Yankees and Viennese like to complain about is in fact not that variable. All weather has a certain zone of consistency. It is variable within a set of invariant boundaries.

There was a great poet in the United States named Robert Frost. He lived in the area of the Northeast United States, which we call New England, and he is our regional bard. He lived mostly in northern New England, that is Vermont and New Hampshire, where the weather is very cold, I would say it is just below sub-alpine, so it is the kind of weather you might have on an Austrian mountain, not at the top where you have an Alpine zone, but just lower down, and he farmed in this very cold area. In one of his poems he describes a feature of our moral, psychological life, as well as of biological life on the planet:

> . . . though there is no fixed line between wrong and right,
> There are roughly zones whose laws must be obeyed.

The example he gave for this phenomenon was his peach tree. Peaches typically grow around Virginia, which is approximately 800 miles south of his farm. He dared to transplant this peach tree to the colder zone, and as he is writing this poem, a bitter northwest wind sweeps into New England from the Canadian arctic. The storm brings wind and snow and very low temperatures. Robert Frost is sitting in his house looking at his peach tree thinking, "It's going to be frosted. The buds are going to be frozen solid and it will die." And then he asks, why are human beings always trying to do something new, creating something new? If I left this peach tree in Virginia it would be a healthy tree. Of course *I* wouldn't get any peaches from it. But I transplanted it to this cold zone. Why? Because there is a chance it might live. If we didn't have such a cold storm, maybe it would have lived. There is no clear line where peach trees can survive. "But there are roughly zones whose laws must be obeyed." You can't plant a peach tree in Greenland, nor in the tropical Caribbean, but you can give it a try in New England. This is a rule of our psychological and moral life also. When we look at the concept of karma, and we ask, "What did I cause, what is happening to me in my life, I am not aware of having caused this or that; I don't know what I can or can't do that is correct or proper" . . . "There's no fixed line between wrong and right / There are roughly zones whose laws must be obeyed."

I had an example of this just the other day. A young woman came up to the lectern after a talk about Vipassana meditation in Germany, and she said, "I've just taken a ten-day Vipassana course. It was absolutely excellent. I would like to continue this meditation the rest of my life but I have come upon a moral problem. I am a relatively poor person. I can't afford to buy organic food, which is more expensive than regular food. But I feel that if I buy regular vegetables, they've been sprayed, the spray has killed insects and I have taken a vow not to kill as part of my life as a meditator, so I am breaking my vow. What should I do?"

I told this young woman a story from the life of the Buddha, where he teaches Vipassana to a young meditator. In those days there were no meditation centers, so people would just go off and sit at the root of a tree where it would be shaded. India is very hot, so in ancient India when a Buddha was teaching, he or his students would sit in the shade under a tree. This young meditator was very enthusiastic; he went off to meditate; he went to the root of a tree and looked down and he saw a lot of insects and ants, and he thought, well, I better go to a different tree. I don't want to kill any little bugs. He went to a different tree. There were some worms, some caterpillars and he said, I should try a different tree. If you have been to India you know that it is a tropical country, teeming with life. Everywhere that young meditator went all day he couldn't sit down for fear he would break his vow and kill something. At the end of the day he returned and the Buddha said, "How was your meditation today?" The new student replied that he couldn't meditate because he couldn't find a place that was free of insects; he couldn't practice Vipassana for fear of breaking his moral vows. The Buddha clarified for him that there often is no clear line between right and wrong. You can't be so rigid in your morality. Do your best. Try not to kill anything. Try to keep the vow. But to turn the vow into a fetish that cripples you and prevents you from even being able to meditate is making a clear line in a world of moral and ethical zones.

Scientifically, poetically, morally we struggle to find precision in a world of fluidity. Between not-trying and defeat, and its polar typology of rigidity and unrealistic expectation, we find the middle zones: lawful to some extent, variable to some extent. We can predict weather three days ahead, but not a week ahead; we can try to plant peaches in Northern counties, and they may survive some winters but may also be killed; and we meditate without waiting to first attain moral perfection or saintly *ahiṃsā*. The first principle of a more complex science is that, often, even when things seem as variable as weather, they actually are controlled within a range.

The second principle, which is really another way of framing the first, is that there are phenomena in nature called attractors. The common example is a magnet. There are also attractors on a planetary or cosmic scale, magnets of the universe. The climate is attracted to the zone of plus 45°C, minus 45°C; something is attracting and magnetizing the planet to that zone. There is a theory that the ice ages, or the ages of great heat—when there were giant ferns in the middle of the United States and Europe—that these climates happened when the attractor changed. We may be in a change of attractors right now. Personally, I hope not!

Now, what contribution does it make to our meditation by our pondering complexity, weather, and attractors? This is very important to a meditator, if we are trying to live a life of awareness of what we are causing. The *Tathāgata* tells us to be aware of what we cause and what causes us; it's the heart of the teaching. But as soon as we close our eyes, we become aware that there are so many problems on our minds. Every person is dealing with economic problems, health problems, political problems, social problems. Even if you have pleasant friendships, a functional family, you still have some problems in your friendships or in your family. When you close your eyes and start to meditate, many, many problems come up on the surface of your mind. You are supposed to be observing your sensations and being aware of change, and instead you are thinking, "Why did he say that to me? He's such a jerk. I'm always nice to him and yet he says nasty things to me. That's not my karma. I didn't cause it. It's his fault. He's the one who said it." And so this struggle goes on, to understand how to create a good life for ourselves, a peaceful mind, free of this anger, blame, and feeling of a mind running down a track of unhappy thinking.

There was a Buddhist monk about fifteen years ago who criticized Vipassana meditation and said that it can't be the teaching of the Buddha, because we each have so many problems that you can't get through to the end of them. How could the Buddha ever have gotten through all his problems? All humans have problems. Even the Buddha had problems. How could he have gotten through all of them one by one by one? The Buddha says that we live millions of lifetimes. Think of all the problems he or we accumulate over so many lives! How did he sift through or transcend all of them while he was sitting there meditating? You would have to meditate for millions of years to get rid of all your problems.

Now I would like you to consider the fact that meditation and the understanding of karma are based on the scientific reality of attractors. That means that when you meditate, sometimes your mind becomes attracted to a problem, which then seems to occupy your whole life. The classic example is a young adult is trying to figure out, "What should I do with my career? How should I earn my living? Do I want to go to this kind of school or to that kind of school?" And that conundrum becomes a strong attractor. It occupies his or her mind like a bulldog at the front door of thought. Nothing can get past it. Now imagine if meditation, and the meditative way of life, and the Buddha's way of life, all become one strong attractor to you. Just as the weather is held within a band of temperatures, once you become organized around a strong attractor of the teaching of the Buddha, your whole life is held within the zone as described by the Buddha as the right way to live. In that moment of insight, decision, and commitment, hundreds of problems may disappear. Many moral dilemmas may evaporate once you have guidance. Many questions about how you should or shouldn't live may be solved. So meditation resembles weather, first, in that it gives life an organizing principle within certain bounds without rigid rules. Second, it can help you reorganize your life around a strong attractor that holds you steady even though there is no fixed or rigid point. It isn't even a matter of being rule-bound or obedient. It is a matter of meditating in such a way that your life becomes organized in a swirl of activity that rotates around zones and realms of morality and reality as revealed to you by the vows and meditations themselves.

Let's take an example of how something can be organized, yet fluid. The first law discovered through meditation is that everything is changing. How can such an unstable world be organized? Let's think about sports. If you are watching a football game, there are certain fixed rules. They've got lines. If the ball goes out of those lines it is out of play: the game progresses and is ordered by fixed rules that define zones of play. Every day on this planet there must be a million football games going on. In Latin America alone, there are probably 900,000 every day. Every little kid in India, also, every little kid in all of Europe is playing football. What a thought, to jumble them all together and see just how much energy is being burned daily by the mass of boys and girls kicking a soccer ball all over all of our continents! Here is the amazing part, the complexity-science part, the reason this analogy is helpful to our thinking about karma: they are all playing by the same rules, and every single game is different! There are no two games that have ever been the same, through all the innumerable fields, and lots, and dusty yards and playgrounds, decade after decade. There is constant change, constant variation within fixed limits, within fixed rules.

> . . . there is no fixed line between wrong and right,
> There are roughly zones whose laws must be obeyed.

Modern science, poetry, or football, reveal to us that the universe consists of both fixity and fluidity, laws and freedom, karma and chaos, simultaneously. We have freedom to choose, and our choices will have consequences, but there may well be many variations upon that sequence of choice-and-consequence.

Another principle of complex causality is the importance of very small effects and how they might become magnified to very large effects. This phenomenon has been popularized. Many people have heard of the so-called "butterfly effect" which is not a real event. It's a metaphor, an example. The metaphor is that a butterfly flapping its wings somewhere over the Indian Ocean creates a little bit of turbulence in the air. The turbulence creates a change of temperature. The change in temperature creates some convection currents and the convection currents create some winds and the winds travel across the ocean and get stronger, and as they travel further they get increasingly strong over the vast expanse of the ocean; so once these winds get to South America they form a storm. Allegedly there is a connection between this butterfly's flapping its wings near India, and a storm off the coast of Brazil. That's not to be taken literally. It's a metaphor for how small effects, magnified by other events over time and space, may have a larger than expected impact.

This apparently irrelevant example can be used to highlight something that is very important in the life of a meditator. Vipassana meditation, the teaching of the Buddha, is based upon a strong commitment to live a moral life style, and the Buddha emphasizes being very careful about your personal morality. Why? Some little tiny deviation, how much will that hurt? If I shoplift a small little thing, how much will that hurt? In the United States we have these mega-stores, these giant chains like Wal-Mart and I have heard that sometimes young people rationalize, well, if you shoplift from Wal-Mart, I mean Wal-Mart's gross annual income is probably worth more than most nations, so their wealthy stockholders won't miss a few pennies if I take something on "a five-finger-discount." Who gets hurt by that? But the answer could be, there might be a butterfly effect. The harm to consider is not the minute one to the balance sheet of the New York Stock Exchange. But what about in your own mind? Who can say that these little variations, these little permissions that we give ourselves to deviate from the ideals we wish were true on this planet, how will they effect our own habit patterns, our own cynicism, our own idealism, our own treatment of other people?

The butterfly effect may not be observed externally, financially, but internally and psychologically. Now we can see the *Tathāgata*, who sees causality everywhere, like a scientist of complexity, weighing in on all sides of complex phenomena, advising the young meditator not to be so obsessed with morality that he can't sit down under a tree for fear of hurting an ant; but also advising us to be vigilant towards our own quotidian ethical actions, because over time and place, they form the basis of our Pacific Ocean or of our stormy Atlantic.

There was a good story about two convicts who were in prison. The first convict says, "I was put in prison because I broke some moral rules of society, I have been punished for that. I recognize that I made a very big mistake, and when I leave prison, I won't do this again. It was a butterfly effect. I made a small mistake and I ended up with a ten-year prison sentence." The second prisoner vigorously disagreed: "When I get out of here, I am going to do the exact same things. I didn't make any mistake at all. The problem was, those other people set their ethical standards artificially high."

Complex causal thinking reminds us to consider variation within limits, the strength of certain attractive variables, the long-term ramifications of minor deviations, and another one: multiple effects from the same action. I saw this very frequently in my life as a psychiatrist. It's one of the complexities of human life, the complex phenomena and apparently chaotic phenomena that we have to consider, that the same one trait can produce both pleasant and unpleasant effects in the same life. I witnessed many examples where someone would have a very forceful, charismatic personality, which is often a good thing in the world of business or in professional life. A person who has a lot of energy, a lot of drive behind their personality, is likely to be successful. That same person, however, may well have impaired interpersonal relationships. No one likes to be pushed around by a bully. No one wants to be the friend of someone who is always dominating and controlling. So a trait that works well in business is not necessarily a trait that works well in marriage. Ironically, we often get rewarded for traits in one zone, for which we get punished in another zone. So one form of action can have different impact in different spheres of life.

Yet another complexity: action may not show its effect for a period of time. Frequently, I meet relatively young, relatively new meditators, enthusiastic people who are meditating on a daily schedule, taking ten-day Vipassana courses once a year and making very good progress, very pleased with it, but they tell me, "I have this problem. I came to Vipassana with this certain problem." Let's say, "I'm addicted to cigarettes or I drink alcohol in a sometimes self-destructive way; and I've made great progress but this one trait hasn't gone away yet." That student may begin to backslide due to frustration or sense of defeat. But it may take more time for an effect to be manifested.

Human life is not the same as taking a billiards cue and striking a billiards ball. Sometimes persistence is the secret of making an effect manifest. So we can see that linear thinking: "I did something, and now I want to see the effect," can be inhibiting; whereas complex causal thinking can be very productive. The attitude there is: "I am putting out into my life this effect. Every day I am making the effort to be aware, conscious of my sensations, aware of change, accepting change, observing change neutrally and living an ethical, moral life by which I am attuned to the ramifications of my thoughts and actions. That may not produce every single effect that I want exactly on the schedule that I want it. But why should I give up? Isn't it reasonable to assume that if I keep expressing one causal variable over time, if I keep emitting this signal, that in the long term it will be received?"

Our way of life might well take into consideration the synapse, the time-gap, between our actions and their fruits. Not every criminal is caught red-handed. There are years to attend between planting a peach tree and harvesting. Did you plant your peach tree next to Robert Frost's and was that a good location for peaches?

In old scientific thinking the world was seen as ordered. Maybe some people thought that God orders the world. "Every sparrow that falls, God makes that sparrow fall." That's not a very satisfying theory because that means that God is making all kinds of mass murders, all kinds of extinctions of animal and human life. But some people thought that and found some satisfaction. Other people, more scientific and authentically religious, felt: the world is causal up to a certain point, but there is also chaos, no order, just caprice. We conclude that things are *not* clearly causal. Or they *are* clearly causal. Both of those exist in this world. Chaos exists and order exists.

In complex scientific thinking, which is sometimes referred to as chaos theory, there is not a dichotomy between order and disorder. They are on a continuum. Things can be very ordered, partly ordered, or less ordered. Nothing is totally disordered however, according to scientific thinking. There's some degree of order everywhere. The degree of order is more or less. For example a river that is flowing takes many different shapes. The shapes are somewhat chaotic. If you think of looking at a river flowing past, you see whirls and swirls and many shapes but it is not totally chaotic. You don't see any squares for example! You don't see any oblongs floating downstream. So a river is slightly ordered but relatively less ordered than for example the human body, which is much more ordered.

Today I look like myself. Tomorrow I will look like myself. There is a tremendous order within the change of my body. Some ordering principle is taking bananas and rice and tofu and regenerating a pile of organic cellular matter that always looks like me! We believe that most of that order is coded in the DNA. I don't look like I looked twenty years ago so there is constant change, but the change follows an apparently recurring and self-duplicating sequence. On the other hand, the order not only shows gradual change, from brown hair to grey hair, from size forty-two shoes to size forty-three shoes, but eventually, suddenly, that sequence appears dramatically disrupted. We call it death. No more tofu-and-vegetables-on-rice get added in. Decay takes over. Has the ordering sequence entirely disappeared, as the DNA stops guiding the biotransformation of the cells? Or has most of the sequence terminated, but other, subtler aspects perhaps continue at a level that requires a different angle of observation?

Both a river and a body have degrees of order and degrees of disorder, and both have different amounts of each, and those amounts themselves not only guide change, but they are also subject to change, which we see when a river floods or dries, or when a body exercises or dies. Order and disorder are degrees of each other. They are aspects of each other, or, you could say, they are aspects of one thing. When we look at things that appear to us to be random or capricious, the question is: is there some degree of order, less degree of order than we would like, than we would wish, but some degree of order in this apparent disorder?

A very important example for the meditator to understand is the Buddha's idea of *anattā*—there's no self. Generally we grow up feeling, well here I am. I'm myself. The Buddha never said that we do not have a subjective sense of self. Of course you have a subjective sense of self. But it is not an eternal, enduring thing. It is not an entity. It's not an essence. It is a self-perception, by a highly organized phenomenon, us, that is caused by many, many causes. The Buddha didn't speak in terms of chemistry, physics, or biology, but as modern scientists we think the body is a product of atoms, organized into molecules, organized into cells, organized into tissues, organized into organs and the organs are organized into something we call an organism, that is to say, "I." The level of complexity within each human being still greatly exceeds the possibility of science to understand. It's very organized. But there is nothing within it that is separable from the organization of its components. There is no essence. There is no eternal element. The joke in medical school was that in the old days some early scientists thought that the "soul" was located in the pineal gland, which is a small organ near the brain, with no clear function. It's a little sac in the head . . . maybe that is where the soul is hiding. Today we know that the pineal gland is an endocrine gland that secretes melatonin. So all of you who had a nice rest last night can thank your pineal. We may want to pay homage to our pineals, but there is no soul hiding there. Within the incomprehensible complexity of the human body, there is no hidden soul. The complexity itself is what we are.

If you want to say, "soul," you are referring to the intricate, transcendent arrangement by which our human love and insight animate matter.

There is in us is no thing, no essence that stays free of change. There is no magical glue. What endures is cause and effect, the laws of the universe, from which our organization sprang, and in which our lives have participated, and into which we put back our intentions and actions, to become the next iteration of the universe.

When we look at the world through the eyes of the Buddha's teaching, we see change in everything, we see order in everything, we see lawfulness in everything, we do not see any permanence in material.

There is one more complex scientific concept deriving from chaos theory to help us understand impermanence and *anattā*. Let's consider the "edge of chaos." The most relatively stable, long-lasting phenomena combine order and some disorder. First, a simple example: if you have a society that is heavily ordered, a dictator comes in and says, OK, now everyone is gong to do this, everybody behave like this, if you don't do this, then we will shoot you; that society becomes very ordered, but usually it does not last a very long time. As soon as the dictator dies, everybody rebels and chaos follows. If you take a chaotic society you find a great degree of disorder, and higher level of impermanence. A revolution usually does not last a very long time. There is a limit to how long people can tolerate the disorder. Another strong man may take over to restore order.

But if you take a democratic society, you find the most enduring societies. There is order, there is lawfulness, there are rules, but there is also a chance for change. People can argue, people can disagree, people can vote governments in and out, and you have a mixture of rigidity, that's lawfulness, with fluidity, that's change. That kind of mixture is called "the edge of chaos."

Now, each individual human being is actually a system. Our bodies and our minds are systems at the edge of chaos. We are heavily ordered as I discussed. We're atoms, molecules, cells, tissues, organs, the total organism, vast amounts of order, and yet we are capable of remarkable change. Among the entire biosphere, human beings are the most flexible, able to tolerate high degrees of transformation. We can live in the Arctic, we can live in the Sahara, we can live with heavy clothes, we can live with light clothes, we can build houses, we can live in a vast array of changing circumstances. I am told that people can even dwell happily in New York City. So the combination of complex control and the ability to face newness and go with the flow, follow change, is one of the features that has made human beings the dominant life form on the earth. Who knows, maybe that first dog was correct and it's not necessarily a good thing. Nevertheless, human bodies and human societies manifest that feature, the edge of chaos, where a system is both ordered and chaotic, both capable of stability and capable of change, permitting maximum adaptability.

Now in the mind of a meditator, this also becomes a very striking phenomenon. Meditation on the surface is an attempt to control your mind. When you begin Vipassana meditation you begin by practicing Anapana, which is a form of mastery of the mind. You try to control your mind, by giving it a focus on the breath. So it would appear superficially that meditation is a form of mind control. You say to your mind: do this, meditate on the breath; then later on you tell your mind: meditate on sensations. So the initial understanding is, it is an attempt to impose order and control on your mind. Anybody who actually experiences meditation over ten days will in fact find a mix of two things. You develop a very ordered, focused, clear mind, what's called *samādhi*, and after that you might experience a very wild, stirred-up, daydreaming, visioning, thinking mind. In fact, one of the benefits of meditation is that it permits the unconscious mind to come up on the surface. This is beneficial only if there is a concurrent attempt to maintain awareness, focus, and order. If the unconscious comes up on a very controlled and ordered mind, the control and order helps buffer the creative, changing, varying potential of the uncontrolled. As people meditate, their minds reveal and show this truism of nature—that the greatest wealth of life forms, the most adaptable and adjustable life form, veers on the edge of chaos, where you have feedback, alternation of order and variability. One of the benefits people feel when they meditate is: "Oh boy. I got such a great insight during my last course. I realized something about the way I should live. I never understood that before and when I took this ten-day course, I got clarity finally." These characteristic bursts of fresh insight derive from the mingling of previously unconscious disorder with consciousness-augmented order. Your mind surfaces in all its complexity.

We have spent our time together considering cause and effect, noting how many patterns this one relationship can take, and applying that to our own lives, to rid ourselves of narrow, mechanical science, which would make the reality of karma absurd and unacceptable, and instead opening to the best of our own Western scientific traditions, which breathe new life into the insights of a *Tathāgata*, revealing the webs and chains and synapses and patterns by which causality permeates the world.

The last feature I want to discuss is the complex attitude toward order itself. To me this is the most important and is the one I found most satisfying.

When I began to enter into the world of meditation, I heard for the first time about unbounded time and space. All of Western thought is based on a bounded sense of time and space. "In the beginning, was the word." Or, "On the first day of creation..." Well what about before the first day? When was it, was there time, no time, then where was it? And then Western time is also based upon a last day, a final day. If it is religious, it is a day of judgment. What about after the last day? There's nothing. Well where does everything go?

The sense of time and space in the Buddha's teaching is without any horizon. There's no limit. The Buddha says either there was no beginning or, if there was a beginning, there's no point in you thinking about it. It must have been almost infinitely long ago, and is not your problem. And there's not going to be any end. Or if there is going to be an end, it is going to be almost infinitely far into the future and your thoughts and actions and insurance policies will have been canceled by then. There's no point in you thinking about it. As far as any human can honestly say they understand, there was never any beginning and there's no visible end. Nor is there some place where, if you go far enough to the left, everything stops. Or if you go far enough to the right, you fall off. All any honest human can say they know is that there is no beginning, there's no end, there's no horizon. There's no limit. One of the most important features of causality in the teaching of the Buddha is that causality continues. We don't know how long it will continue. And we don't know from how far in the past the causality within us has originated.

In Western science we say we are a product of genetics and the environment. And genetics came from our parents. But actually the genome is fairly constant even back into bacteria. The sequence and pairing of bases that form the genome in DNA were laid down in bacteria (or even before that, in even simpler life forms), who are clearly our relatives, and who share the same causality, the same inheritance as we do. At the very least, and with the most rigorous Western scientific thinking, we have to say that all of us are carrying genes that are about a billion years old, and are carried forward from bacteria. Of course there is a great debate about where our genes come from and if there is genetic material outside of the genome, say in mitochondrial DNA or in viral RNA inserted into our genome. That's too complicated for us to solve right now, but we can say simply that, in a scientific sense, each person is a product of billions of years of serial cause and effect, cause and effect, cause and effect. We are preparing a world that will go on for billions of years. We are preparing it. The world is being bent through us. We are shaping it. Naturally each one of us has a very small impact. The bacteria who created the genome didn't know how important they would be. I doubt any of them were fantasizing that they deserved the Nobel Prize for their contributions to biology

The causes of who we find ourselves to be are set on a "long bead chain of repeated birth," as Robert Frost called it in his poem, "On a Bird Singing in Its Sleep":

> It could not have come down to us so far
> Through the interstices of things ajar
> On the long bead chain of repeated birth
> To be a bird while we are men on earth

Our agonized questions about ourselves—"Why is this happening to me?"—may require answers that sweep into the purview of these ancient creatures, answers that can account for a long sweep of history. If someone says, "What does it matter if I make a little error here or there, what does my life matter?" Well, the world is now being passed through us. We are the lens through which living forms are passing. We are temporary, there is no enduring self in us but there is an enduring impact. We have no idea how far that impact will go. We don't have absolute control but there are roughly zones whose laws must be obeyed.

I have spent many years trying to walk the Path of the Buddha, and trying to understand it, too, without surrendering myself to formulas, beliefs, or religion. When I read the old Suttas in the two thousand five hundred-year-old Nikāyas (collections), I glimpse murky peripheries through a lens that has yellowed with age. But even after such a long bead-chain of cultural transformation—leading from the Gangetic Plains at the dawn of recorded history, to our digital, post-modern age—I also see that the core of the teaching shines like new. How can a flash of lightening stay brilliant so long? Part of the "modern temper" that shines in the *Tathāgata*'s words is his appreciation of causality and multidimensional complexity. For those of you with a need to pin your thinking to an intellectual source—and I was warned that Vienna houses a lot of scholarly Buddhists—I would steer you towards the Abhidhamma, or more reasonably, the Comprehensive Manual of Abhidhamma, available in English through the toil of the Buddhist Publication Society. In this most revered and technical presentation of the Buddha's ancient teaching, we are admonished to understand "*kamma*" in the manner that I have presented it today, with no single cause responsible for a single effect, but complex conditions producing complex effects. We are taught to see forces augmenting each other, diminishing each other, canceling others, enabling or impeding others, originating recently or ages ago, now ripening quickly or slowly, emerging obviously or subtly in fine layers of the mind, during this very lifetime, or long into the future, or never again.

The real life of meditation includes, but is not complete with, mindfulness of sensations in the moment. Vipassana, as taught by the *Tathāgata*, constitutes a lifelong path, which emphasizes awareness of one's own volitions as initiators of causal sequences. We act in freedom, and we create our future and also a tiny corner of the future of the endless world. Similarly, we are inheritors, from the past, of long chains of causality, already in play. The path emphasizes awareness of choice, action, responsibility, a charismatic call to a well-woven life, though the starting points of each moment also include ". . . a long bead-chain of repeated births."

Karma is not a fixed doctrine of explanation, such as: "It is god who makes every sparrow fall." It is a stimulus to acceptance of our inheritance, good and bad, like the weather. It is a reminder of our power over our own moods, beliefs, attitudes, future. Karma is a vehicle for asking ourselves thought-provoking questions. It is an encouragement to let go of simple explanations. It is a reminder to stop placing our own demands upon the time scale or the dimensions of personal change that happen to us via our meditation practice. Karma reminds us to let go of wish and worry as much as we can. Karma is recognition that cause often consists of everything intriguing and multifarious, like a football game, the results of which cannot be limited to one kick in the third quarter.

The *Tathāgata* said that our greatest inheritance is whatever caused us to be healthy, free citizens who have the option to walk the path. He also said that the only treasures we can take with us are the compassion, wisdom, and peace that we have stuffed into our own backpack.

The poet Robert Frost was also very funny, and whenever he said something, he usually said the opposite. He was a mature and ironic commentator. In one of his poems he recorded a moment when he was looking into a delicate flower, and in the flower was a spider who had captured a moth and all these little lives were tied up together. Peering over this scene, Frost found it inspiring. To describe this scene he created a phrase that the order, the design of the universe, is for "darkness to appall." It's almost a religious idea although it is put in a metaphor. He was looking at the details of the tiny unknown lives of insects and he wrote:

> What had that flower to do with being white,
> The wayside blue and innocent heal-all?

What brought the kindred spider to that height,
Then steered the white moth thither in the night?
What but design of darkness to appall?—
If design govern in a thing so small.

Every event that is happening to each of those little lives was caused by a previous event, which was caused by a previous event, which was caused by a previous event. There is a sequence, the origin and termination of which defy human knowledge. This does not argue there was some smart old Designer in the sky. But darkness, randomness, and meaninglessness alone cannot account for these lives. They seem to spring from "…design of darkness to appall."

The Buddha said: supposing a person was lost in the woods that had no order, no meaning, no purpose, darkness, completely lost in a dark woodland. He thrashed around for days trying to find some way out. He couldn't find any direction. But suddenly one day he stumbled upon a path, a good path, a wide path well trod by wise men and women of old and he followed this ancient path, and it led him out of the trackless wilderness, He came to a palace and to a city where there was a wealth of grass and water and beautiful buildings and adequate food. The Buddha said, I have been, like everyone else, a person lost in a meaningless, disordered wilderness. But I have stumbled upon this ancient path that has been walked upon by the wise men and women of old. Now I have pointed it out to you, and you yourself can walk out of the darkness.

Questions and Answers

University of Vienna
November 24, 2007

Q: You use the term, "good life." What do you mean by that? I'm mostly interested in the word, "good." What is the definition?

A: That's an important question because there are so many value judgments about what constitutes the "good" life. The concept of karma might apply to a bad life as well. If you are interested in creating a bad life, you can systematically organize yourself around creating a bad life! But when I say "a good life," I mean a life that produces in oneself and in those around one, a feeling of joy, peace, and compassion. That means social concern for others coupled to personal equanimity. Equanimity means peacefulness and harmony. "Good" in Vipassana terms means: "Do what helps others. Don't do what harms others. And purify your own heart."

Q: What is the relationship between free will and causality?

A: There is a long philosophical debate in the Western world about free will versus determinism. If things are caused, if every sparrow that falls from a rooftop does so due to the will of a god, then I have no free will. If a god is going to determine the details of everything that happens, what difference does it make what I do? Even if I imagine that I am acting freely, actually, some god is really both determining my behavior, and even determining my subjective fantasy that I am freely choosing to act in that way. This absolutist determinism forms the basis of some religions, which emphasize predestination, and also of logical positivistic science, which views the world as a machine. Free will is the opposite belief, that I have the power to do anything I want. I create myself. "Existence precedes essence." I am free to determine the essence of who I am. This is the basis of most religions, which see humans as having an option to choose between good or evil; and also is the basis of existential philosophy.

As for Vipassana, it helps us to see that entire debate as a false dichotomy As long as your thoughts are based upon terms like, "free will," or, "determinism," your understanding is constrained by a pre-existing false division of reality. It's like a question; did Buddha favor Apple computers or PCs? From the standpoint of meditation, these speculative conversations do not lead to wisdom or to well-being. Instead, the pragmatic, psychologically wise, and meditation-based answer is: "There are roughly zones whose laws must be obeyed."

You do not have total free will. I can't suddenly decide to become an eighteen year-old African rock star. But within those zones there is freedom of action. I can be a thoughtful and effective sixty-two year-old American. I have degrees of freedom within degrees of constraint. There is a beautiful image for the relationship between freedom and absence of freedom within one zone. Emerson, who was a nineteenth century American writer, said he often felt that he was trapped in a rock cave. Many things weighed down upon him; history, government, health, illness, wars, politics. He was just one little man. He couldn't control almost any of the vast network of conditions that surrounded him and which determined the quality of his life. They seemed fixed in place like a rock cave. But, Emerson said, in a flash of insight, when a human being fully and deeply understands the basis of life, there is a burst of freedom, as if he could take his hands and for one second mold the walls of rock around him.

Insight, said Emerson, is a cosmic force entering in and operating out from the human mind. However, it is occasional and momentary. Many other causal forces also determine the shape of that rock cave. In context of the concept of karma, this is a way of understanding that carries us beyond false dichotomies of Western philosophy based upon an opposition between freedom and determinism. Karma helps us to locate in each moment the conditions we are to wisely accept, as well as the degrees of freedom we possess to reshape our world.

Q: Is there a point in trying to find out why something happened? How does Vipassana help you find peace of mind?

A: This answer is similar to the last one: understanding karma should help us find a middle path and to exit from confining artificial dichotomies. If we live a dichotomy, we might say, you should try to figure out why everything has happened to you. With this attitude, you will constantly be stewing: "Why did this happen?" The peaceful equanimity that meditation can bring will elude you. As we have been discussing, causality has gone on for, let's say, a billion years, which is just a metaphor for a vast era of time. And we have been discussing attractors, time delay, multiple causality, etc.

We cannot always fully resolve the details of causal forces in each event. But, on the other hand, if we don't try to figure out why things happened, we will not be able to fully live a responsible and awake life. We will not assume full awareness of our role in shaping our destiny. Therefore, "though there is no fixed line between wrong and right / There are roughly zones whose laws must be obeyed." Get rid of that artificial dichotomy between "understanding" and "accepting." There is a time and a place for everything. When we meditate, our volition is only to focus our attention on the arising and passing of sensations. We intend to do nothing else. We make no other willed effort. We do not try to analyze causality.

However, other things do happen during meditation. Anybody who meditates—a guarantee, written guarantee—anybody who takes a ten-day Vipassana course, anybody who keeps on meditating over time, will get many moments of clarification about why things have happened the way they have happened.

These insights rise up unwilled. They are the surfacing of residues of the previously unconscious mind. If you try to force clarity, only your conscious mind will be involved in your meditation, which will then remain superficial. If you just try to meditate, the conscious and unconscious together will bring up new awareness of why things happen. Without any willed effort to try to find out why something has happened, you find your insight deepening.

Q: Suppose I want my meditation to become my strong attractor? How can I do that?

A: It is possible to change a strong attractor. Unfortunately, if we use climate as an example, there are now climatologists who think that is exactly what we so called civilized humans are doing on planet earth. For example, (I hope this is not true, but it is just an example to explain) if the climate goes up one or two degrees, the people who don't care about climate change say, "so what? What are one or two degrees?" But if the Greenland ice cap melts, then there will be less ice on this planet and there will be more water. Since there will be less ice, there will be less cold air. Since there will be less cold air, there will be less preservation of ice, and there will be more water. Not just the temperature may change, but the temperature-regulating mechanism may also change. A vicious cycle may occur and the attractor, around which our entire climate rotates, may change. We may have a radically different climate. In that case, the dogs may have to open the refrigerator for themselves.

Going back to our interest in meditation, we can create not just a new behavior or practice, but a new strong attractor in our life. Continuous long-term effort can create a positive cycle, mutually reinforcing itself at the various levels of meditation and action. If you make meditation important in your life, and thereby come close to the teaching of the Buddha at the experiential level, not merely at the thought level, meditation will become more important to you. The practice and the insights will reinforce each other. As meditation becomes more important to you, you will meditate more, and it will change your life in a good way. The practice, insights, and behavior changes will reinforce each other. Going back to what "good" means, this newly deepened positive cycle may make you more harmonious and peaceful inside of yourself, may make you more compassionate towards other people, or may make other people experience you as more harmonious and peaceful, a positive psychological and social cycle of well-being. As this happens to you, you will appreciate your meditation more because you are getting so many benefits out of it. So you will meditate more seriously. And more benefits keep flowing out of it. The way to make meditation your strong attractor is to take it seriously and enter yourself into the serious meditation courses and come out and live a good life with meditation on a daily basis. Starting with volition and determination, meditation will become your strong attractor, and you will then effortlessly rotate around it.

Q: Is karma going to continue until we end our ego? What does enlightenment mean to you?

A: Yes. Karma continues until we end our ego. However karma, as we have been discussing, has different strengths, or, to use a scientific word, valence. Karma has different valences. The Buddha was born with some karma. He took birth, from his past karma, but, through Vipassana meditation and from walking the eightfold path, he released his old karma and generated no new karma, so he realized *Nibbāna*. That means he did not come back in any karmic form. So yes, karma continues until we end our ego. The word, "enlightenment" can be approached from two sides. Enlightenment is actually an English word that English language translators applied to the Buddha's language, and in the Buddha's language he says, *Nibbāna*. He realized *Nibbāna*. *Nibbāna* has two meanings. One meaning is that person is not capable of negative thought and behavior. Negative means hate, ill will, cruelty. So that person is now incapable, not just that they are holding themselves back, they are incapable of those sorts of thoughts and actions. Another way of understanding *Nibbāna* is: going beyond the material world, transcendence of all limiting stuff and things, understanding that there is nothing to cling to, affirming no mode of being. Those are the two meanings the Buddha gave to the word *Nibbāna*. It's a little far away from our daily experience. But it keeps us mindful of our continuing potential to grow in positive ways, to grow in love and peace.

Q: How is it possible to live a moral life with a bad condition of the mind?

A: We all do that! One of my heroes in the United States is a nineteenth century American writer named Thoreau. Thoreau created the concept of passive resistance that Gandhi adopted. Thoreau was a very beautiful writer, a nature poet, and I admire him greatly, but Thoreau said, "I've never met anybody as bad as myself." And I have learned something similar through meditation. It is easy to lapse into judging other people, thinking "They're bad, I'm good; they're jerks, I'm wonderful." But when I meditate, I realize I'm just about like all the people I dislike. I'm similar. I probably conduct myself differently, but inside of every human being unless you are some very wonderful Buddha, inside of all of us are the common weaknesses, and immoralities in our fantasy world. So we all have a weak and selfish mind. But we can do exercises to strengthen ourselves. Even the Buddha had to do that. He is described as working very strenuously to develop his virtues and his mental condition. I think Vipassana could be understood as a form of exercise the way people go to a gym, lift weights, or run, to improve their aerobic capacity. Vipassana is an exercise that increases our identification with a good life.

Q: Many young people want to know what is the sense of life?

A: That's very important. I agree. That's why I ended with the quote from the Buddha saying that he too had been lost in the wilderness. So whether you take the Buddha as a literal person or as a metaphorical example, the Buddha's life starts out as being lost. There's actually a discourse in the ancient Buddhist texts that describes the Buddha being just filled with anxiety and dread. It says, "anxiety and dread!" This is very different than most people's stereotype of the imperturbable stone Buddha. All of us start with dismay, existential dismay. What is the meaning of life? Vipassana meditation doesn't give an exact answer, like: "The meaning of life is—go shopping at Wal-Mart for Christmas;" or "The meaning of life is that when you die you float in the sky with a lot of little fat cherubs with wings."

Vipassana is a mix between existentialism and realism. Each person finds meaning to life when they feel filled with love and peace. A lot of our dismay is because we feel bad. The American novelist, Herman Melville who wrote *Moby Dick*, said that most of organized religion is simply the product of indigestion. A lot of philosophical angst is actually emotionally driven. When you are feeling good, a lot of existential dismay dissolves. When you fill your heart with a feeling of well-being, meanings fill you. They may not be permanent meanings, they may not be abstract, eternal, philosophical meanings, but in every interaction you find a meaning. If there is an elderly person walking across the street in front of you and they slip on icy pavement and fall down, you don't ask, "What is the meaning of life? Let them fall. Kick them." You reach out to pick them up. You don't ask the meaning of picking them up. When your life is a series of well-being for you, and goodness for others, that existential dismay isn't answered philosophically, but it does dissolve.

Q: In modern psychotherapy, we are encouraged to react by giving expression to certain problems, while in Vipassana you are taught not to react and you are told to observe your reactions with equanimity. Is there a contradiction?

A: There is a slight contradiction but not as big a contradiction as this question would imply. Modern psychotherapy is not one thing. It is very variable. There are many techniques and practices. There are many different forms of it. I hope that there are no psychotherapists like the one implied by this question, who encourage their patients simply to react. One of the tasks of psychotherapy is to help people to modulate their reactions. Emotional modulation is one of the keys to being a mature person. Problems are best expressed in a skillful manner, at the well-chosen moment, and in a thoughtful way. But it is true that Vipassana emphasizes observation and equanimity and provides a specific and unique tool to do so. I think of psychotherapy as a valuable help for people with specific kinds of problems who need particular help. It provides particularized, one to one, professionally attuned, unique listening and response. It is designed as a treatment for problems, not as a path that leads to a long-term practice with equanimity as its focus. Vipassana is organized somewhat differently, has a different focus, and is uniquely embedded in a path aimed towards *Nibbāna*.

Q: You speak about zones. Does that mean if a person has a habitual pattern such as fear, anger, etc. they can only change to a certain extent? Or can they completely eradicate these?

A: That is a key question for all of us. If I have some problem, can I really get rid of it? Or will that goal lead me into perfectionism and frustration, and I would be better off just accepting a lessening of it? In complex thinking, you get both answers! The answer is: it depends on the person and the problem. And that person with that problem doesn't know their own outcome either. We will have to assess two different factors. First, there are zones of causality, there are strong attractors, things tend to stay within the zone.

Second, we also discussed the butterfly effect, the potential to magnify small effects. Janet Browne, an English historian of science, who is now at Harvard, has written a two-volume biography of Charles Darwin that now stands as the definitive biography of that monumental thinker. In the conclusion, Dr. Browne says that the essence of Darwin's legacy is the importance of the small. Tiny changes in a bird's wing, tiny changes in an insect's antennae: evolution is the aggregation of ongoing small events. Robert Frost said, "the long bead chain of repeated birth." So there are very small things that grow and grow and lead to incredibly dramatic changes that shift the entire biosphere. The triceratops and Shakespeare and Janet Browne and Charles Darwin and sparrows are all products of the accumulated powers of the small. That's one side of complex causality.

Another side of complex causality is that some things stay within their zone for a long period of time and not much can move them out of their zone. There is a strong attractor there. But, we have also discussed time, a generous sense of time. That was a breakthrough that Darwin absorbed from the Nineteenth Century's new science of geology, but which had been present in ancient Indian thought back in the days of the Buddha.

There will be many iterations of the equation that is you. We don't know all the answers about our future, what we can change, what we will have to accept. When people talk about egolessness, it sometimes gets confused with a shuffling false modesty: people saying, "Oh, I'm so modest." That's really not egolessness. That's pretentiousness. I think real modesty, real humility, real egolessness, is the ability to learn. You have to accept the fact that you have been ignorant, or wrong, in what you had been thinking up to now.

When we ask ourselves, from the base of Vipassana, from a standpoint of egolessness, am I stuck with this problem, can I only grow to a certain extent, can this be like a butterfly effect, small changes that will catalyze a revolution, the answer is, "I don't know!" There is something to learn. But, "I don't know"—authentic open-mindedness—is very different from a negative conclusion. The most destructive thing we can do for ourselves is to reach a negative conclusion, such as: "I know I cannot change. I know that." You do? You know that far into the future? You know all the variables that are going to affect you? You know the entire impact of a life-long meditation practice? I think you don't know. The answer is, we don't know. With that, we keep on walking.

Q: In psychology the ego is very important. How do you think of this as a psychologist and a meditator?

A: There is confusion in the term, "ego" that derives from translation problems. The word has two origins and two different meanings in English. When Freud was translated from Viennese German into English, the word 'ego' was selected by James Strachey, a British translator. This "ego" refers to a cluster of psychological phenomena, including both the sense of self, but also the organizing and executive functions of personality. The "ego" in Freudian psychology is a larger concept than the subjective sense of self. It is a positive, necessary part of adult function in any time or culture. There is no word "ego" in the teaching of the Buddha, because the Buddha of course did not speak English. The Buddha used the word *attā*, which means a permanent soul that feels like our "self." The Buddha discovered through his Vipassana practice that there is no permanent "soul" or "thing" that is enduring within us. We are transient, impermanent, and *anattā*. The prefix "an" means "without," without attā. Unfortunately, the term, *anattā* got arbitrarily translated into English as "egolessness." This has created confusion as if Freud teaches us to have a strong "ego" in contradiction to the Buddha who teaches us to get rid of "ego."

The Buddha never said you shouldn't have a strong organizing personality. On the contrary, he said that we should all develop a strong sense of determination, strong wills, a definite sense of choice and effort. In the Freudian sense, the Buddha teaches us to have strong "egos" but to realize *anattā*. The Buddha was never falsely modest. He didn't say, "Aw, shucks, I'm not really the *Tathāgata*." He was forceful, self-directed in taking steps to organize his life. He lived in an alert, focused, precise way. He lived with a sense of urgency. It's true that there are some aspects of western psychology where a certain kind of aggressive dominance is sanctioned, that I don't think a meditator would cultivate, but actually it is important to remember that as meditators we are not getting rid of our volition and our diligence. The Buddha said the single most important virtue that a person needs to walk the path is diligence. So getting rid of ego does not mean getting rid of effort, focus, will-power, determination, or a self-directed, energetic life.

Cultivating Inner Peace

A talk given at Milltown Institute
Dublin, Ireland
December 3, 2007

I am going to be talking to you about cultivating inner peace from the standpoint of a logical or educational position. Inner peace is something that we are not generally taught about; it is not on the scholastic curriculum. We don't study it in schools, and yet it is a skill, a knowledge, a capacity that can be understood and developed.

Inner peace is a topic that interests a certain kind of person, someone who feels there should be more to life. William James, who was the great Harvard philosopher and psychologist at the turn of the twentieth century, said, "Religion is the area of the More." Although inner peace is not exactly synonymous with religion, it fits into that spiritual realm of the "more" to which James was referring.

There is a story my father liked to tell about three young men who came to the United States as immigrants to pursue the American Dream. "The American Dream" means making lots of money, having cars and houses and excess income to spend. These three hopeful friends might have come from any one of the countries of Europe, quite likely from Ireland, because this story goes back to the great wave of immigration from Europe to the United States during the earlier part of the twentieth century. It turns out, in the story, that one of the men was typical of the American dream. He was a relentless hard worker, he had no sense of humor, he had no fun in life, but he pursued wealth to excess and he indeed became a multimillionaire.

The other two fellows hung out together as friends. They argued a little, they played some sports, they enjoyed life, they appreciated the quality of the day and they remained poor despite the promise of America. They lived well, but they never fulfilled the Dream that led them across the Atlantic.

As you might guess, the strenuous first friend, who became a multimillionaire, died young of a heart attack. And when the executors opened his will they read: "I've got a lot of money and I am not giving it away to anybody. People say, 'You can't take it with you' but I am going to prove them wrong. Take everything I earned and convert it into bars of gold. Then put the gold into a giant pot and melt the gold until it is liquefied. Then take a new Cadillac car (in America, particularly in those days, the Cadillac was the status symbol, the proof of having "made it," the Jaguar or the BMW of its place and time)—take that Cadillac and dip it into that gold cauldron until the whole Cadillac is solid gold. Then raise it out of the cauldron and let it congeal until you have a solid gold Cadillac. Then put me in the driver's seat and bury me at the wheel of my solid gold Cadillac!" Well, it's the law, the executors have to follow the will, so that's what was done. Money was converted into gold, gold was put in the cauldron, the Cadillac was dipped in. And finally, as the dead man is being lowered into his grave behind the wheel of a solid gold Cadillac, his two friends are watching from the graveside. One of them turns to the other and says, "Man! That's living!"

So, we're going to be talking about the realm of the "more." There's more to life than life.

Is everyone familiar with *The Lord of the Rings*? Frodo, the unlikely little hero, who is assigned by fate to free Middle Earth from evil, but who is as helpless as any of us, quotes his mentor, Bilbo Baggins, as saying something like this: It looks as if there are many roads, many highways, many paths in this world. But actually, in this whole world there is only one road. It is like a great river. All the streets and avenues and highways that we see are simply tributaries to that one road. And the springs that nourish all those tributaries begin at every front door.

The cultivation of inner peace will only seem realistic to someone who feels option and opportunity. To direct our life towards an infrequently realized ideal, we have to have confidence that the springs of life are right in front of us, and not in some unreachably remote mythical destination.

Walt Whitman, the quintessential American poet, said, "Afoot and lighthearted, I take to the open road. Healthy, free, the whole world before me, the long brown path winding before me wherever I choose. Henceforth I ask not for good fortune, I myself am good fortune . . . for now I see the makings of the best persons. It is to grow in the open air, to eat and sleep with the earth . . . the whole world is an open road."

There is more to life, an adventure, a direction, an intrinsic and beckoning movement forward. We can go somewhere. Good or evil depend upon us. Joy or sorrow can enlist us in their forces. We can be active agents in bringing peace into our hearts, into the world. The Buddha said, "I have been myself a lost person. But I have found the path trod by the wise people of old. And now I can point out to you this path."

Wherever we turn we find this archetypical image of a path that leads out of the wilderness of confusion, out of the thickets of "Work, Consume, Die," to a "more" treasured by the wise. It was the Buddha who made this archetype central to his teaching. His legacy, he said, was the re-discovery of an ancient path, leading out of the brambles of emotional distress and intellectual dismay, and ending in the columned halls of wisdom.

The first step on this path is recognition of our common heritage about the cultivation of inner peace. For thousands of years people have groomed different fields of expertise. Most of what we have to cope with in life is not new, but a repeating pattern. Somebody has already thought about how to build strong buildings or how to cultivate and grow good food or how to run a good government. And there have been thinkers for thousands of years about how we can find inner peace. One component of the answer that is universal and found in each of the quotes I mentioned from Tolkien or from Whitman or from the Buddha is that people who seek inner peace always have some affiliative response to natural environments. Human beings tend to feel more peaceful in natural environments.

There are many poems that capture this but one I like is by Pablo Neruda, a Chilean poet of the twentieth century who wrote in Spanish. He died in 1973 shortly after he got the Noble Prize in literature. Neruda was born in sparsely populated Southern Chile where he developed an intimate rapport with forests and rain and seashore. When he was growing up in the early twentieth century, Southern Chile was an almost uninhabited country. That long skinny nation extending down the west coast of Latin America goes all the way to the wilds near the Antarctic. Neruda also was strongly influenced by the traditions of Asia, because as a young man he was sent by the Chilean government to be a Consul Officer in Sri Lanka and in Burma—two countries that share Theravada Buddhism. Pablo Neruda learned to experience nature from a culturally enriched viewpoint. In lines from one poem, Neruda said (as translated by Alistair Reid):

> suddenly I saw
> the heavens
> unfastened
> and open,
> planets,
> palpitating plantations . . .
> riddled
> with arrows, fire and flowers,
> the winding night, the universe.
> And I, infinitesimal being,
> drunk with the great starry
> void . . .
> felt myself a pure part
> of the abyss,
> I wheeled with the stars,
> my heart broke loose on the wind.

I particularly like that poem because when I was in college there was a whole literature about European philosophers, predominantly the French philosophers, who always felt nauseated when they contemplated the abyss. Maybe they were huddled in Parisian basements far from real trees and stars. Yet here is Neruda delighting, "And I infinitesimal being . . . felt myself to be a pure part of the abyss. I wheeled with the stars."

This sense of peace that comes from nature is spangled through the canon of world literature. Nikos Kazantzakis, the author of *Zorba the Greek*, wrote a beautiful Haiku-like poem about this fusion of nature and peace. He said in his autobiographical musing, *Report to Greco*:

> I spoke to the almond tree and said,
> "Sister, speak to me of God"
> And the almond tree blossomed.

But there are two problems with seeking peace in nature. One problem is that it makes us dependent upon an external presence. We find peaceful nature when we look at the stars at night or when we feel communion with the almond tree or when we wander the open road of the world. But we don't find this peace in ourselves, so there is a bit of dependence, or, you could say, there is the passivity of waiting for grace. You don't feel peaceful, but at a propitious time and place, Nature might deliver it to you. Obviously there is no moral failure in that, but there is something limiting.

Another problem with finding peace only in literature and only in nature is that human beings, each one of us, contain another dimension. We human beings are a biological phenomenon, an animal, a mammal, adapted for survival. If we didn't know how to survive, we wouldn't be running and spawning over the globe in such profusion. The way that human beings have endured and dominated the earth is quite remarkable. We can survive in many types of climate, we take over the jungle, we appropriate the wealth of the oceans. We are very excellent at adapting and surviving. We are, after all, predators, that is, we are take-ers. We eat the nutrients that have been grown by other living organisms. We are like smart wolves with two hands and a feeling of entitlement. Our predatory, survival oriented, adaptive nature is very self-serving and self-justifying. First we claim we are big peace seekers, we want "more," we don't want to be buried in a gold Cadillac, we want to take to the open road with Frodo and Whitman and the Buddha, but there is a part of us that doesn't want to do that at all, despite our claims. We want to be safe. We want to be secure. We want something that we can hold on to. The gold Cadillac is a ridiculous hyperbole but we want to be able to say, "I got this, I'm safe, I'm comfortable. I don't want to wander on the open road with Walt Whitman who says he doesn't need any good luck because he is just all happiness and good fortune. I want a job. I want a house. I don't trust in fortune."

So the human agenda is divided. Most of us who say we want inner peace, if we look carefully at ourselves, what we actually are saying is, "I want inner peace but not too much of it." Or, "I want inner peace but not at the risk of what I have already aggregated." Or," I want inner peace but I don't trust this world. I don't trust other people. Human beings are dangerous. Bad things do happen. They could happen to me."

There's a story about us humans in the Garden of Eden—a variation of the story you already know—based upon a different picture than the one you've heard about before. There are Adam and Eve, leaving the garden, while a giant hand points down at them, gesturing, "Get out of here!" You can tell that this is transpiring after the Fall, because Adam and Eve are ashamed. They are covering themselves up. But in this story, instead of just leaving in shame, as they are said to have done in the Biblical story, there are two angels who are watching the whole scene, unlike the way it is told in the Bible. And the two angels are talking. One of the angels says to the other, "You know, I think one day He is going to regret having made this impulsive decision to reinject these two organisms back into the environment."

Human beings are dangerous. Human beings can be destructive. We are all human beings who are participating in globe-icide. So our question now must balance out two opposing directions. How can stealthy, strategic predators, like us, also give peace a chance? How can we remain competent and skillful, but still, as the Buddha put it, "lay down the rod"?

There was a period of time when I set about the task of studying people who attained inner peace. What do they say? How did they do it? There are people from every era of history, every culture, who address this problem in one degree or another. Here is a conclusion that seems timeless and culture-free: there are two agendas that human beings share. One agenda is to be peaceful, to be happy; "I want to find 'more' to life." The other agenda is safety, security; "That gold Cadillac may come in handy, or gold may come in handy, you can't trust other people, history is perfidious. There could be a war; I better situate myself in a good position."

With two apparently competing agendas, a very idealistic or simple philosophy might conclude: "Well, just walk the open road." A very pragmatic or very skeptical philosophy would say: "Make sure you know which side your bread is buttered on." But notably successful peace seekers throughout time and place have come up with what psychiatrists call the end of splitting. Splitting is where we divide human life into antagonistic partial answers. The end of splitting is where we make complex whole answers that take away divisiveness and produce skillfully integrated middle paths. The middle path of inner peace is to live a practical, competent, skillful, worldly life, during which every moment is also infused with the spirit of harmony and peace. Peace is part of survival, not its antagonist. Rather than dividing or splitting adaptation and harmony, you fuse them.

Successful lives of inner peace exemplify competence illuminated.

Almost every human being is born with the capacity to hear sound. We have an organ that is attuned to the vibrations of sound. Almost every human being is born with a capacity to see light. Our eyes are receptor systems for the vibrations of light. So even though there is a potential for human beings to be destructive and dangerous, every human being is also born with an organ whose function is to receive vibrations of inner peace that actually already exist in the universe just as light or sound vibrations preexist our perceptions of them. Whether we feel it or not, vibrations of peace and harmony, just like sound and light, already exist.

Why don't we receive these signals more often? Why do we feel dependent on literature, on nature, or other people? Why are we relatively blind and deaf to the peace that is woven into the tangled world? Why are we so divided and struggling every day? To some extent science provides us with an answer to this question. Einstein said (this is a paraphrase): many people believe that studying science makes you cold. These critics imagine that the scientist sees the universe as dead, just a collection of stuff following fixed laws. It has no spirit in it. But, Einstein said, my experience of studying science has been just the opposite. I have come to realize that most people are fixated upon themselves and the events very close to them, like an optical delusion of consciousness, as if we were wearing lenses through which we could only see very near to us. This becomes a shackle, a blindness, a myopia to the full nature of reality. Einstein said the goal of human life is to become emancipated from the shackles of myopia, to feel increasing compassion not only for the living beings near us, but compassion that reaches out to the whole universe. Einstein continued: when I looked out into the universe with the wisdom and insights of science, I felt myself reduced and humbled by "the grandeur of reason incarnate in existence."

I found that quote remarkable. Einstein isn't taking the limited position that he discovered laws of nature, or that laws guide nature, or that lawfulness exists within nature. He said that nature is the manifestation of reason. Nature emerges out of reason. Reason is incarnate in existence. That's not a casual commentary. He was an Einstein.

There is a sense in human beings that inner peace is as much a lawful part of the universe as is reason. We intuit that, we wish it were true, we feel it is true, and yet inner peace is so elusive, so intermittent. We feel dependent upon outer sources. We experience holy peace in childhood and then we lose it. Our days have become so frantic. How can we get away from this frenzy and live a life in which we are following the tradition of fusing together our practical, canny lives, our adaptive, constructive, safety-oriented, mammal-like nature, with our spiritual, peaceful, harmonious, nature that feels and believes that there is something "More"?

Successful peace seekers of all eras not only put an end to splitting the sacred and profane, but they do so by the tool of ethics. The morally awakened life is simultaneously skillful and sacred. There is an irony to this. We do ethical things out of selfishness. Wanting to feel better ourselves, we set constraints on our conduct, even on our thoughts, on behalf of other beings. But again peace, in fact all mature, integrated, synthesizing mental traits, derive from a middle path, rather than a split. A split would say a person is either altruistic or selfish. In reality, we are both, not in series, but simultaneously. We are altruistic because we are selfish and our selfishness makes us recognize the mental poise and balance that springs up from altruism. This principle was labeled by the historian of religion, Mircea Eliade, as the conjunction of the numinous and the ethical. The numinous, what you feel is holy, what you feel is sacred, is always conjoined to the ethical.

Trying to be good, to feel good, is critical, but not enough. It is necessary but not sufficient for the cultivation of inner peace. In my own life, and in the lives of quite a few other people in my generation who were looking for a way to connect to inner peace, there was a felt need for a skill, something you learn, which is ethical, and yet is more than the practice of the ethical, more than reading good books, more than looking at the beauty of nature and feeling at one with the stars. There is a need to clean, to purify that mental organ of inner peace which is analogous to hearing and seeing, but which is not guiding us as clearly. That organ is fogged, "a kind of optical delusion." Along with competence illuminated, along with morality, we can learn how to see perceptively, hear acutely, and purify our minds to receive peace.

I first came upon Vipassana meditation in India where it was being taught by my teacher then, and my teacher now, Mr. S. N. Goenka. He was busy spreading Vipassana around the world, teaching ten-day residential courses in which you would learn this skill. Vipassana is an education or a training that is a natural and logical extension of observing the lawfulness that is in nature, our own inner human nature, using one's own body and mind in the way that a Neruda or Einstein used the stars or external nature.

A number of things stood out to me about these courses, and made me interested in them.

The first thing was that they are taught for free. Vipassana is a spiritual transmission, a person-to-person transmission, in which something is given away for absolutely no reason except to help somebody else. I describe it as being like the trees. All day the trees are creating oxygen and at the end of the year we do not get a bill from the forest, O.K. you owe us 1300 Euros, and there has been inflation so it is 1350. We get starlight every night, or many nights from the stars (probably in Ireland there are only a few nights you get star light among the clouds!) and at the end of the year you do not get a bill from the stars for their having illuminated the night. Vipassana is like the trees, like the starlight, something that is distributed for free. People help in any way that is available to them, helping to conduct a course by cooking or arranging the course site. Even the teachers are merely very experienced volunteers.

A ten-day Vipassana course begins with each person taking a commitment to live by ethical vows not to kill, steal, lie, use intoxicants, and for the ten days you take a vow to abstain from sexual activity; that's for ten days only. You are also asked to spend ten days in Noble Silence. Noble Silence means you use the silence to develop yourself, without reading, don't fill your head with words, no writing, you are asked to surrender any writing tools, no computers, no cell phones. The most intrusive and problematic annoyances of our society are taken away from you and you are free to spend ten days just meditating. In this Vipassana course of silence, of ethics, of being in a quiet location, you are taken care of, you are fed every day, and all you have to do is meditate.

The goal of the course is to learn to locate peace within yourself. The introductory meditation is on your breath going in and out. You can think of it as learning to read a treasure map, "Here is where the trail begins to get me to where inner peace is buried." You will learn in a period of ten days how to locate inner peace not just in nature, but in your human nature, because after all we are part of the stars, we are made of atoms and molecules; why shouldn't we be as inspiring to ourselves, as filled with inspiration, as Neruda felt looking at the heavens?

As you begin this meditation you are trying to locate inner peace and you're taught: just start meditating on your breath going in and out.

The first thing that happens to anybody who tries this simple exercise is that, instead of feeling inner peace, your mind explodes. It explodes with thinking and with daydreams and memories and worries. The classic thing is that someone sits down and feels: "Finally ten days, I closed the door. There is no phone. I've taken a vow of silence. I'm going to live without killing or stealing, or lying. It's going to be totally peaceful." Then the first thing they think is, "Oh, my God. I've left the burners on the stove! I didn't lock my door! Where did I put the car keys? I forgot to tell someone to feed the cat."

As you practice this meditation—a very simple form of watching your breath, objectively, without trying to add anything to it—over three days of practice, you move from craving stimulation, to being increasingly comfortable with yourself, observing nature within. You experience yourself for the first time, at least momentarily, free of wishing and wanting. Maybe it is a second, maybe it is ten seconds, where you are just sitting still, observing your breathing and those ten seconds represent a total revolution in your life. You are released from desire or demand or fear. In the past, even when we were going to sleep, trying to relax ourselves, typically we added in some daydream, some stimulatory hope: "When my vacation comes I will be sitting on the beach, I will be very peaceful," and then we fell asleep. Vipassana meditation is a complete break with the habit pattern of auto stimulation or external stimulation, and opens an entryway into a path of peace that is pure peace, observational peace, peace that comes from the mind that isn't being stirred by the winds of mental life.

The next six or seven days of a ten-day Vipassana meditation course consists of observation of the nature of one's own body as one can observe it through the sensations of the body. There is a deeper reason beyond the mere neutrality and acceptability of this focus, and that is, to eliminate mind-body dualism. Instead of my mind meditating by thinking about some object, a vision, some belief, some idea, I am meditating simply by observing the reality of my own nature -- the very same nature that we stand in awe of, that we find so beautiful and inspiring, or what we are always looking for outside of ourselves, as if "It" is nature and "We" are here in our brains peering out at nature. That dualism is eliminated by Vipassana. We are nature observing nature. Our minds are nature, our body is nature. Nature is integrated with watching nature. You practice experiencing yourself from within as different sensations arise and fall. By sensations I mean anything. It could be hunger; it could be stiffness in your back. But there are many sensations, and I will describe that more in a moment. The first thing that happens when you commence Vipassana on day four is another storm of thoughts and feelings, just as happened on day one, because the body is filled with sensations that are very meaningful, important, and often previously unknown. We are bodies and minds that consist of a vast storehouse of constantly shifting sensations, and our long-practiced, unconscious tendency has been to constantly react to them with desire and fear, wish and rejection.

Unhappy memories are stored in the sensations of the body. One reason we become alienated from our bodies is to avoid those unhappy sensations. Alienation is caused by aversion to unpleasant sensations that we have been carrying around inside ourselves. When we meditate honestly and directly, observing sensation, it's true that we have to confront unwanted things. We have to learn to observe the sensations neutrally and peacefully without reacting to them. One reason that we like to observe the stars and not observe the beauty of nature in our own being is that the beauty of nature in our own being does contain unwanted things.

There are many other sensations stored in the body. One of the remarkable things about learning to systematically observe your body is that you become aware of a vast array of sensations for which there are no words in English and I would say there are no words in any language. Our bodies consist of numerous, varied, subtle, constantly changing sensations. We are like rivers. Every moment our bodies are doing what chemists call biotransformation. We take foodstuffs, protein, carbohydrate, trace minerals, zinc, and we change them around and we make a human. Every day we are remolding ourselves; every minute we have to refurbish and reanimate that human. Every microsecond and millisecond we are scintillating in constant, incessant biotransformation, and when you meditate on the sensations of your body you come in contact with this river of flow and change. It is not random. My foodstuff is making me. Your foodstuff is making you. We are observing natural law. There are patterns, there are sequences, there are meanings, there are memories, there are thoughts, there are feelings connected to all the sensations. Body and mind are the same thing.

Typically when we are reading a book we are unaware that our thoughts are inside our body. We feel that we are thinking thoughts in our brain, which we falsely experience as a detached airy entity. When you meditate systematically and continuous-ly—those are two key words, "systematically" and "continuous-ly"—you become aware that every thought changes your body. In fact, if we go by modern science, we say that thoughts are the flow of neurochemicals. Probably everyone is aware of modern psychopharmacology. By changing the level of serotonin in people's minds, we change their minds. Actually, anyone who has ever drunk a beer in a Dublin Pub knows the same thing. You change the chemical nature of the brain and you change its thoughts. Anybody who has ever been hungry knows the same thing. You're hungry, you're irritable, you are having some testy thoughts, you eat, you feel relaxed, you feel better, your mood changes. But this is actually always occurring at a micro-level, at the level of tiny chemical changes in the brain, the brain be-ing in the body, neurotransmitters being in the embodied brain, so we are mind-bodies, a hyphenated term, constantly changing. We are dynamic, scintillating, ordered, coherent aggregates that move from birth to death.

And it may well be that coherence, synthesis, causality, and sequential, lawful change, which Einstein says is embodied in the entire physical universe—it may well be that all of these manifestations of lawfulness continue after our death. Why would it be that causality goes right up to death and suddenly the universe becomes a-causal and molecules start bouncing around randomly? Actually—if you think there is something as absolute and final as death is often construed to be—then you are being non-scientific, since the essence of the scientific world-view is continuity of causality. Everything is caused by something before it. Everything that exists will cause something after it. If there has been an event, there will be a sequence. Of course some events have a very short sequence. You draw a line in a bathtub with your finger and that sequence lasts a tenth of one second. But as I like to say, I live in a very beautiful, little pastoral town in New England; it's very green and pretty, and everybody who sees it says, "How can you be a psychiatrist here? People here have no problems." But a victim of every war that has been fought in the twentieth century has entered my office. Those wars have not gone away. They will actually never go away as long as there are people who continue to suffer from the residues of violence. When Yugoslavia was breaking up, one of the causes was a previous war that had been fought one thousand years ago.

A few minutes ago I proposed that there is an organ in the human being whose function is to receive the vibrations of peace, in the way that the eye receives the vibrations of light. You can challenge me, "Ok, if there is an organ, where is it? Is it in the toe? Is it in the ear?" The answer is: that organ is the integrated whole person, who becomes attuned to peacefulness the way that eyes formerly shut, but now opened, are receptive to light. To open your eyes, so to speak, to this inner peace, your meditation must contain two features: it has to be continuous and systematic. Systematic means your awareness has to cover your whole body, not just some parts that you like and you leave out other parts that you don't like; and continuous, continuous over time because the body is changing, so if you just observe it for an hour it is a very partial, inauthentic observation. You need to observe it continuously. Ten days is an introduction, an immersion in this cosmic reality manifesting within the universe contained within your own skin. If you have awareness moving through your body systematically, continuously, and you are just observing without reacting and craving, you awaken a new aspect of your human potential. You feel increasingly peaceful within yourself. You learn a skill of how to relocate that peace through meditation.

The experience of Vipassana is based upon the material world, but it isn't necessarily limited to the material world. It is true that everything we can observe in the mind and body is based upon this flow of particles, these sensations, the serotonin, the brain chemicals, the body chemicals by which we think and feel. But it also may well be true that there are things that we can't think and feel, that are beyond ordinary sensation, and that those also exist.

Now, I had one great objection to learning meditation. I was a child of the sixties; I am someone born at the end of the Second World War, and I grew up with a very strong commitment to positive human action. People should do something. People should change the world for the better. Nikos Kazantzakis, whom I quoted earlier, when he was speaking to his almond tree and it spoke back the way trees do, Kazantzakis said, "Woe to the youth who begins his or her life without lunacy. And what lunacy? Every human being should try to do what has been considered previously to be impossible."

All of us want to build a better world, bringing to fruition something that hasn't existed yet. So I was very skeptical of meditation that makes you feel good. "That's nice. I want that. I feel I need more inner peace. I would love to learn that skill that those Vipassana people teach, but doesn't that meditation make you passive? Isn't it narcissistic? Isn't it solipsistic? Doesn't it take you out of the world?" The answer is, as a person meditates and gains inner peace, automatically, without any additive new factor, that person wants to get up and give peace and harmony and well being to other people. As soon as you begin to click in to this learned skill of how to find more inner peace, the first thing that starts happening is an inspiration, "How can I bring this forward in my work?" "How can I stop getting so angry at my sister and share some of this peace and harmony that I am getting?" "How can I find a profession in which I can use this peace and harmony constructively in society?" It is an automatic event that happens; that is to say, the essence of wellbeing is the desire to share itself. If you are a socio-biologist, you could say human mammals are social mammals, and when they have something beneficial for the pack, it is to their our own advantage to share it.

I had a professor in college who was a great hero. He was a Quaker pacifist during the Second World War. He went behind enemy lines, into Nazi occupied Europe, and was feeding orphans and rescuing people whom the Nazis were pursuing. Naturally he was captured and imprisoned himself. Despite being starved, he survived, returned to the USA, and became a college president as well as an anti-war activist. Yet he acknowledged his own struggle against despair about the number and the magnitude of our difficulties. He said, this world is so complicated, it has so many problems, it is impossible to figure out what we should do in life that is good. People want to feed orphans, but then they want to improve the economy of their country, then they want to stop global warming; how do we know what to do? He said the only way out of the purposelessness of life is, "to find the warming fellowship of other seekers of the truth." As soon as you are in that fellowship, your perplexity evaporates.

The Buddha said, I've taught so many things, I've taught so many people to practice Vipassana meditation, but actually, the ancient path, the path where wise people walked, the entire path is friendship with the wise, friendship with the good. The Dutch poet, Lucebert, said that human life consists of the journey from being forlorn to finding communion.

Rabindranath Tagore, the Indian Nobel Laureate poet, was a meditator, not a Vipassana meditator, but he said:

> You and I have floated here on the stream
> that brings from the fount at the heart of time
> love for one another.

The Buddha said, all of us should live like cows—in India cows are a very positive thing—cows with a calf. Everybody we encounter, every situation we encounter is our calf. Each person is potentially able to take care of a situation and the person next to them. Our American poet, Robert Frost, said each person seems to be moving freely through the world, but if you examine your heart, each of us at our best, is like a silken tent standing in a field:

> bound by countless silken ties of love and thought
> to everything on earth, the compass round.

Questions and Answers

Milltown Institute
Dublin, Ireland
December 3, 2007

Q: What distinguishes Vipassana meditation from other forms of meditation?

A: That's a very good question. There's no hierarchy among kinds of meditations. I have tried to avoid any sense of better or worse, right or wrong. So the issue is just how do you distinguish one from the other? What are the defining features of Vipassana, and might it be helpful and acceptable to you. The hallmarks of Vipassana are as follows:

Number one, it is taught for free. It's not a business, commercial, or even a professional enterprise. Number two, it is non-sectarian. Anybody can practice it. It doesn't matter whether you have, or don't have, any particular religious or philosophical belief. Number three, although it is non-sectarian, it is ethical, based upon a moral code of conduct. It is not mere expediency. It appeals to someone who has enough confidence in human ethics to lead a morally guided life. Number four, it's taught in formats appropriate to the technique itself. It is not taught by anyone, anytime, without regard for its integrity and depth. We have a ten-day course but the essence of a ten-day course is for systematic and continuous observation, which differentiates Vipassana from meditation that can be taught in an hour or even a weekend. Finally, number five, the thing that is most salient about Vipassana is the emphasis upon observation, neutral observation, continuous, systematic, neutral observation of sensations of the body. So it's an integration of mind and body—mind observing body itself—and observing the body means observing it at the level of the sensations without craving or aversion. That's Vipassana.

Q: Give us some Yeats!

A: The poster for this public talk mentioned Yeats, but I became intimidated about an American quoting Yeats in Ireland. I thought to myself, "Probably everybody in this audience has got a PhD in Yeats. You all might have started memorizing his poetry when you were three years old." Of course, such a poet comes from the whole world and belongs to the whole world. There's some evidence that "The Wild Swans at Coole" was influenced by Indian poetry. Yeats was the man who brought Rabindranath Tagore, the Indian poet, to world fame, which eventually lead to Tagore's Nobel Prize in literature in 1913. Yeats fathered him into English language recognition, and after that, in 1915, Tagore wrote a beautiful poem about wild swans; so it is interesting that Yeats also has a poem on wild swans, written two years later in 1917.

The general view of Yeat's poem is that it is a melancholic reverie upon death. There are nine and fifty swans upon the lake. Yeats sees them return annually, but understands that someday this sequence will run out. He will pass away, and the scenes of nature around him will also fly away, disperse. He says, "I've looked upon those brilliant creatures, and now my heart is sore." So the poem commences with a melancholic tone. But I find that the ending of the poem shifts in a surprising way. I imagine that the poem describes an awakening from sadness about time and loss, to an acceptance of them. Yeats comes around to peace with age, changing nature, change in himself, change in the birds, so the last lines say:

> Unwearied still, lover by lover,
> They paddle in the cold,
> Companionable streams or climb the air;

Their hearts have not grown old;
Passion or conquest, wander where they will,
Attend upon them still.

But now they drift on the still water,
Mysterious, beautiful,
Among what rushes will they build,
Besides what lake's edge or pool
Delight men's eyes when I *awake* some day
To find they have flown away.

(The italics have been added for emphasis.)

Q: How do you stay peaceful when you are being yelled at or confronted? Don't you have to respond?

A: That's right. We don't want our inner peace to be an artifice or a form of passivity, as if—you study meditation, you become a good meditator, and then you become a passive wimp and everybody can push you around and you never stand up for yourself. As I said, I had that fear and I am glad that I had models of people, my teacher and other friends, who are active, competent people, who are also meditators.

One theme that I have come back to a number of times is that we find a misleading tendency towards dichotomization under conditions in which mingling and merging would provide more fertile and adaptive responses. Should we be active or passive? Are we going to be skillful and competent or will we be idealistic and accepting? The middle path, the end of splitting, is to put together two opposites, to form a complex middle that takes the best of the apparent polarities. So when we are being yelled at, typically we think of two alternatives. One is to yell back; defend yourself, stand up for yourself; don't be a wimp. The other simple alternative is to just "take it"; we are meditators; be quiet; let them yell; turn the other cheek. The middle path of Vipassana is to be able to observe your self, your body, your sensations neutrally enough, that you can locate your feelings, not deny them, and not act on them either. With awareness and with pause and poise, can you overcome your fear, your anger, well enough to respond with firm, non-hateful, non-angry, non-belligerent, honest, straightforward, forceful speech? I'm not saying that I can do that all the time. If you are a psychiatrist you work on it every single day, in your psychotherapeutic interactions. If you are a family person, you work on it every single day, in your family relationships. Sometimes I am successful. Sometimes I am not successful. But the goal is neither to yell back, nor to be passive and simply take it. The goal is to find right speech. Right speech is speaking honestly and forthrightly to the issue without being, demeaning, aggressive, provocative or belligerent.

Q: How does one maintain a continuous state of meditation with all our daily chores and life in general to deal with?

A: It is probably very rare that anyone could leave their introductory Vipassana course and maintain a continuous state of meditation in daily life. There almost always would need to be two intermediary steps. The first is that we encourage people to establish a twice-daily meditation practice, every morning and every evening. It is like physical fitness. You stay in shape. Meditation needs to be exercised. The second step is that as people practice meditation over a lifetime—there are many people now who have practiced over ten, twenty, thirty years—meditative skill does begin to enter into even the mundane tasks. So how do you do it? You do it by very long-term development of the practice.

Q: Is being in the present, the "now", essential for finding this inner peace?"

A: I would say a qualified "Yes." I would phrase it slightly differently. I think one thing essential for finding inner peace is integrating with your body, which helps you integrate better with the world. So it's not just being "in the now" in a conceptual sense, but in an embodied sense. Another thing is that the "now" includes the past. If someone was once shot by a bullet, is it still lodged in them; was it removed by surgery; do they then retain a surgical scar? The event happened in the past, but the pain continues to exert its influence now. I want to say something different than "New Age" thinking, which leads people to construct a life of avoidance and denial. Conversely, if someone went to India forty years ago and stayed there for six years then he is still carrying that experience with him. So if we have a sense of the "now" that includes the past and the future, it becomes a pregnancy of experience, aggregated wisdom, and applicable skill every minute. Genesis says the world was created in such a particular place and time, but if you think of Genesis as a metaphor for every single second, and that every second is pregnant both with what has happened and what will happen, then I would say living in the "now," including the now of the body, certainly is germane. This can help preclude irrelevant fantasy, feckless dreaming, unnecessary dread.

Q: Does Vipassana have a role in clinical practice, treatment of depression and bipolar mood disorders?"

A: A ten-day Vipassana course is not something one should launch into at the height of a crisis. You have to sit there in yourself, inside yourself. You do have instruction, guidance, you have a very caring volunteer staff around you, very supportive teaching structure, very clear directions; but most of the day you are sitting still inside your own mind, meditating. When you are heavily weighted down by a mental problem, that's not the time to learn. The example I give is that I personally like to exercise. I've tried to stay fit most of my life. About ten years ago I was hiking in the mountains on a rainy day, on slippery rocks leading steeply downhill, and I fell and broke my leg. Well, that's not the time to join a jogging club. So there are times when one should not launch into a Vipassana course. But that doesn't mean in the future, after you have had a cast on your leg, and your bones have recovered, and you have strengthened it gradually—you don't immediately go out and run five miles—but over time, yes, you get back to hiking or jogging.

Similarly, there are degrees and intensities and kinds of psychiatric problems that may or may not preclude one from taking a ten-day Vipassana course. The way to find out is: one can apply to a course. We have a well-designed system of evaluating and discussing with applicants whether the time is right for them. Sometimes the advice is to wait; you shouldn't take the course now. At other times the advice is: "That is OK; your problem is not enough to stop you." So the answer is qualified and requires information, evaluation, and discussion. In the long term picture of life, however, a person who is working with meditation is cultivating inner peace through their own mind and body, who is helping the community be peaceful—that warming fellowship of the seekers of the truth—we hope that person will be well buffered.

Q: Does imagination help us acquire awareness of our organ of inner peace?

A: Although imagination may make an important contribution to art, and even to hypothesis-formation in science (Einstein said that imagination is more important than information in the genesis of scientific thought), it is not the same thing as awareness of reality, and is not part of meditation. Not that imagination is harmful or that a person shouldn't have a good imagination, but in the long skill of cultivating inner peace, it's more fruitful to practice awareness of reality as it is.

Going back to Einstein—Einstein realizing reason incarnate in the universe—imagination played a role in triggering reflection and exploration, but investigation of reality gave him such a profound conviction. No one else can speak with the conviction of Einstein because no one else has investigated so systematically. So as far as meditation is concerned, systematic and continuous observation of reality is the key.

Q: How can I know that my desire to share or to help isn't just a codependent addiction?

A: Yes, it is true that sometimes we help others as a way of either avoiding ourselves, or as a way of avoiding self-dislike, by constantly trying to get rewards from other people. So it is true that sometimes helping others can hide an addiction to praise, although there are obviously a lot worse problems a person could have. The Buddha gave a metaphor to explain this very point. How should we properly balance self-care and care of others? His simile comes from scenes that were visible daily in the agrarian society of ancient India. The Buddha said that all of human life is like being a cow with a calf. You must feed and nurture yourself; you have to have healthy food or you won't be able to give anything to anybody else. At the same time you have to start giving away nutrition. Whatever you have is only valuable to you if you share it with others. Human beings never feel at their highest potential when they are keeping something to themselves. So the answer is: if you are sharing or helping as an addiction, that means you are giving away milk when you are not feeding yourself well with grass. To genuinely give, you have to have a full tank. Make sure that you do take care of yourself so that you are healthy when you give.

Q: How do I overcome my aversion to doing nothing and to being alone?

A: It sounds as if, for this dilemma, meditation is the ideal rectification. In Vipassana, you don't start out alone. In ten-day courses, you are alone in a room full of people, "alone/together." You have a teacher checking on your progress regularly, and you feel a sense of communion; you are part of a group of like-minded folks. But you are alone with yourself inside your mind. A course helps you develop comfort with being alone with yourself, even though you are not literally alone. When people say that they don't like to be alone with themselves, that means there is something inside you that is troubling you, so you don't want to be alone, facing it without help. When you take the ten-day course you can get through those kinds of inner fears and resistances. You learn to make peace with them in a new way, from a new angle. As I said, everybody has unpleasant things that definitely come up in meditation, and you learn to be with them, to just observe them, observing not your mental problem but observing its physical basis in sensations, which are quite neutral, quite easy to observe. You can learn to be alone with yourself and not have aversion to doing it by practicing meditation. It might take a little while to learn.

Q: Does inner peace go anywhere if a meditator stops practicing?

A: I'm not sure what that means. Does it fly away somewhere? If I close my eyes, is there still light? There was a cartoon I saw about that classic philosophical question, "If a tree falls in a forest, and nobody is there to hear anything, did it make a sound?" In the cartoon, a tree is lying on the floor of the forest, and is thinking to itself, "I suppose it ought to be enough that I myself heard it." So inner peace is a phenomenon. If our eyes are closed we do not see the light. If we go deaf we do not hear a sound. Light and sound still exist independently of our personal sense organs. Inner peace exists. We can come in contact with it. If a meditator stops practicing, the ability to contact it will fade. It's like food. If I ate a really great meal yesterday, do I have to eat today? Not really. Do I have to eat the next day? Not essential, but of growing importance. But after 30 days, that's the end. So you do have to eat regularly. You do have to sleep every day. Hopefully most people study or learn every day. Similarly, you need to meditate every day for it to remain vibrant.

Q: Is meditation just another stimulant?

A: The only active processes during meditation are awareness and observation. Nothing new is being added into the organism's nervous system. No sense organ is being stimulated. So there is a particular quality about the calm and peace of meditation that is different from the very pleasant tranquillization that may derive from the addition of pleasant sensations to one or another sense door. Meditation is unique in its wakeful non-stimulatory awareness.

Q: What are your thoughts on TM and mantra based meditation?"

A: Meditation is an experience, not an idea. It's not a philosophy. You notice there is no philosophy that goes along with Vipassana. It's a way to experience yourself and those aspects of yourself that are most treasured. So we can't really compare meditations by our ideas. We can only compare them by our experiences. I have never experienced TM. Even a brief trial of a meditation is not a fair, deep trial, and would not form the basis for a valid comparison. I have no desire to comment on other kinds of meditation. I hope they augment the amount of harmony around us.

Q: Can you elaborate a bit more on what you meant when you said we are altruistic due to selfishness. Is it our egos that make us altruistic?

A: One thing that the worldview of Vipassana shares with the worldview of psychiatry—and I would say is common sense—is that human beings grow developmentally. Education is culturally designed and sanctioned guidance for personality development. Vipassana is a kind of education, a kind of development, and altruism is a development within personality. There are different contributions to the formation of altruism. Sometimes we are altruistic (like the other questioner implied this evening) simply to please others. As children, our parents teach us simplified imitations of altruism. We imitate that conduct out of a desire to please our parents, or out of a fear of punishment for having failed to do so. Imitative, superficial morality is considered the primitive stage, based upon compliance with authority. This is what is sometimes taught by organized religion: compliance due to fear of negative consequences.

A deeper stage of moral development is called internalization. "Well, I was nice to my aunt only because my mother told me I'd better be, but when I noticed my aunt's smile, I felt really good. Maybe I'll be nice to her again even if my mother doesn't tell me to, because being nice to my aunt makes me feel good." Psychologically we develop from primitive morality to internalized morality. If we continue to practice internalized morality, it may form what we call mature character, for which altruism becomes so much a part of who we are that it begins to spontaneously flow out of us in the way that we speak a certain language. When I am speaking English, I don't have to think about it. It just flows out of my personality. I'm an English speaking person. This is the basis of the simile of the cow with her calf. She takes care of others without thought or desire for reward.

So the three stages of psychological moral development around the issue of altruism have to do with obedience, identification, and maturation. Only someone who cares for others can fulfill their human potential. Character formation in a human being never ends. There used to be the Freudian theory that you developed to a certain age and then you stopped. Today we know that people develop up to the last minute. At the last minute we hopefully will still be living, not just enduring, and we still will be developing, not stuck with who we were. And we will still be learning. That is true for altruism also; it is the ripened fruit of the tree of who we are.

The *Tathāgata*

Faculty of Arts & Philosophy
University of Ghent
December 7, 2007

I have been told that there is a six-hour difference in time between Belgium and New York, but it turns out Ghent is six hours and fifteen minutes different because everything here starts fifteen minutes late.

The famous American Nineteenth Century writer, Henry David Thoreau, said: "The mass of men lead lives of quite desperation." Thoreau described an exemplary alternative, by filling his moments and days with a sense of purpose. For several years he lived by himself in a small, hand-built cabin in the woods on the shore of Walden Pond, where he contemplated nature, read classic texts, and communed with local poets, writers, and woodsmen, and in general tried to elevate his thoughts, expand his feelings, and live the philosopher's life.

It was a revolution for me when I discovered that my American hero was actually inspired by ancient India. On the one hand he was living a life that was available only to Americans. There are few countries in the world where somebody can just go to the woods, find a tamed yet open wilderness, and live in dignified poverty. So it was a very American experiment, and Thoreau is an American icon. But actually Thoreau said that his inspiration came from the great books of India. He wanted space to think and feel. He wanted to live deliberately, so that every day or every minute would be filled with the highest quality of human life, so that every moment would have the brightness of dawn. His favorite adjective was "auroral," meaning, like the goddess of dawn. A light should be steadily ascending in our minds the way dawn comes up in the morning. But his example was not easy to follow. Most people do not want to run away to the woods, or live mostly alone. Thoreau was also an exceptional literary genius, with rare inspiration, concentration, and knowledge. I wondered, is there some other way an ordinary contemporary person can overcome a life of quiet desperation?

Another avenue to a life with an apparently higher purpose is to create a belief or a fantasy that there is someone else in the sky. This someone else has created the universe, and although the universe is several billion years old, and contains a hundred billion galaxies each containing one hundred billion stars, somehow all along he had you and your life in mind. He was creating a cosmos all for you. That scenario is satisfactory to many people, and it makes them feel important and valuable, but to me it was hard to extend credence to the idea that there was some other personality living above me in the sky who took a few hundred million years to create humans through slow evolution by way of slimy things, but who is now very interested in me and in giving my life meaning in Amherst, Massachusetts. It seemed that that must be my own job, the discovery of realistic, intrinsic value and purpose in the context of a vast universe.

At various historical moments, different cultures seem to specialize in creating a new potential or a new kind of knowledge. It is quite amazing for an American to come to Europe, to a city like Ghent or Freiberg or Vienna, where I have been on this journey to facilitate the spread of Vipassana, and to see Gothic cathedrals. We have no authentic Gothic cathedrals in the rough new nation around Walden Pond, though of course there are modern imitations. Here in Europe, gradually over centuries, cultural knowledge evolved the ability to create a cathedral wall which is not structurally required to hold up the building, and therefore can be made of glass. The building is held aloft by buttresses, and the wall becomes an art gallery, a space to decorate with beauty. In all other forms of art, light hits the object from one or another angle, but in stained glass, light is the object of art which the artist has filtered, strained, and shaped as it transits through the glass. An entire wall of stained glass turns sunlight into stories, faces, colors, and floods of feeling. As you stand under the high Gothic vault, and bend your neck back to look up, the prismatic illuminations possess uplifting and celestial quality, a "heavenly light." This artistic discovery, based upon science and architecture, was an invention unique to Medieval Europe.

While I was studying in college, I found out that there had been a time and a place where a culture had specialized in thinking about how to escape from a life of quiet desperation. That time and place was India, two to three thousand years ago. Of course every culture has had buildings and every culture has tried to decorate their buildings, but only medieval Europe had the patience, inventiveness, and inspiration to transform a huge wall into ruby and golden shafts of electrons. Similarly, every culture asked the questions: what is life about, how should we live, how can we live a good life? But only India specialized in answering this question from every conceivable angle.

Historians have tried to figure out why this particular time and place developed this specialty. Successful agriculture freed people from survival oriented tasks; a benign climate reduced the necessities of life; a poetic and speculative tradition extended back beyond our ability to trace its origins; but still, it is remarkable that about two-thousand-five-hundred years ago there was, already well embedded in Indian culture, a group of people who spent their whole lives focusing on the questions: what is the best way to live, how do human beings achieve happiness, of what does wisdom really consist, what is the meaning of life? They not only spent their lives on this topic, but society supported them economically, and respected them for their efforts. They focused on this question free from pre-existing religion. They were not prisoners to threats or promises from an entrenched, economically driven, theocratic power structure. In

India two thousand five hundred years ago, there were no organized religions. There were plenty of religious rites and rituals,
there were a plethora of religious beliefs, but there was nothing
that we could call today organized religion. By organized religion I mean an agreed upon, sanctioned, formatted, codified and
enforced pattern of thought and ritual, something where people
agree which text is a scripture, which person speaks on behalf of
the system, which building we worship in, and what beliefs are
beyond doubt. No one in ancient India was being burned at the
stake or sent to a dungeon for what they did or did not believe.
Instead there was the opposite; a fertile and chaotic melange, a
woven dialogue of people thinking about, discussing, wondering
about, and practicing different paths, different ways of being.

In particular, there were large groups of people who were
called "wanderers." These wanderers were supported by alms
and lived in a university without walls. (In America there is a
trend to call adult education "university without walls". Back
in India it was a literal truth that there were universities without
walls). Someone who felt he had something to teach would sit
under a tree in a park at the outskirts of a city. People could approach him and ask: "What do you teach? What is your philosophy? What is your practice? If I follow your teaching, what will
I get out of it?"

One of those wanderers left a large body of teaching, both
verbal and behavioral, still available to us today, which describes
existential breakthroughs, in the way that the Gothic cathedral
was a breakthrough in luminous art. Like the cathedrals of Ghent, his spiritual edifice continues to attract people today. He
was known by many appellatives, but the commonest name by
which he referred to himself was "*Tathāgata*," a title that has no
meaning for us today. The syllables mean, literally, "Thus come;
thus gone," not very evocative. But *Tathāgata* was his chosen
tag. It has an intensely compressed signification. We could start
by saying it means: someone who just came into the world and
passed out of it again. He just came and went. Don't we all do
that? But *Tathāgata* adds two things. He is someone who has

understood the nature of reality, who can express reality, un-contaminated by his personality. Reality passed clearly through him. He passed clearly through it. He is just and only awake and clear to the facts. He understands "thus", without any "spin". When he speaks, the meaning of truth is revealed. He is not embellishing, adding or denying anything. He has no point of view. He experiences accurately. Second, he leaves the world without any attachment, without any complaint, without any problem. He leaves as unencumbered as he entered. He isn't trying to bend anything by his entry or his departure. He has no vested interests, nothing to prove, no wishes or fears. The truth about life emerges from him and can be more clearly apprehended for his having passed through, and he himself is not in tension with the way things are. He enters "thus": he speaks "thus", and he departs as he came and as he spoke, "thus". He manifests and speaks for reality as it is. That's a very long explanation for a few syllables, *Tathāgata*: thus come, and thus gone, emerging from the universe without any torque and disappearing back into it without pollution, a spokesperson for all of those galaxies and electrons, as natural an occurrence as one of them.

An American folk singer, Woody Guthrie, wrote:

> We come like the dust
> And we're gone like the wind.

And what was it that the *Tathāgata* found, that enabled his momentous claim that he spoke for reality, for the universe?

Well, most of the wanderers believed and practiced similar things to the common beliefs of today, or of all times. Some lived what we call the "*carpe diem*" lifestyle, which is the main philosophy of modern America: we should enjoy life by generating as much sensual pleasure as we can: eat, drink and be merry. Another group of wanderers were serious people who focused on life's difficulties and problems: we face so many things; disease, war, and the petty daily obstructions and deceptions in society around us. Life is suffering and we should detach ourselves from it. The more austere, the more aloof, the more we can control ourselves and not give in to pleasure, the better off we will be. We suffer less if we are tougher. A kind of "tough-guy" attitude towards life was very common amongst the ancient wanderers. Historically, utilizing the bridge of peoples and cultures created by the conquests of Alexander the Great, these attitudes reached the Mediterranean and eventually were written up as the Stoic philosophy of Rome. Some of the wanderers had more spiritual or religious practices: If you have faith in certain things, you can then be happy. They would attest to what happens after death, where your soul goes and whether you do or do not have a soul, or whether it floats in the sky. Many of the wanderers were ritualists. They said that if you practiced a certain ritual, if you burnt a fire and put butter in the fire, or sacrificed an animal like a horse, the gods would be pleased and like you and give you in return a lot of sons and money and you would be happy.

But a few of the wanderers were meditators. Meditation as we think of it today was discovered in ancient India among this group of wanderers. Meditators believed that if you sit still, close your eyes, and concentrate on some internal mental object, you can obtain peace and harmony. Anybody who tries that even for a second will see that to some extent, within the very first second, it works. When life's worries press down upon you, you close your eyes and you start turning your attention to your chosen internal object. When I was a child and we were worried, we used to say: "Count sheep. Pretend you see sheep jumping over a fence." For a second or two seconds or three seconds your worries will go away. There were many foci of meditation designed in ancient India—sounds, words, mantras, thoughts, pictorial daydreams—that were all ways of focusing your attention away from your problems onto some other object. And when you do that, you feel relative peace and harmony, and the more intensely you do that, the more intensely you are removed from the world of problems. Meditation meant *jhānas*: intense concentration on altered states of mind. It was and still is used as an exit door from the overwhelming distress that we all have experienced from time to time.

Though a few people practiced this mental internal concentration with success, there were problems with it. Most people cannot practice it with any benefit at all. If your life is bent on gaining increased concentration in meditation, how can you live? How do you earn a living? How do you have children or family? So, people specializing in this kind of concentrative meditation had to live in remote isolation, in order to concentrate internally, and to diminish distractions from external situations and problems.

You can gain concentration for ten seconds, a minute, an hour. If you are living alone in the jungle, maybe you can concentrate for hours at a time, but eventually some of your problems will break through. And you will have more problems than you had before. You are sitting there obsessing about one thought, one idea, one image, and you are solving no real problems in life. And when you open your eyes, you have more problems than you had when you started this internal concentration. You haven't been active, you haven't adapted to the realities around you. So meditation was practiced, but it was practiced by a few very tough people. It can be seen as systematic avoidance coupled to determination and isolation. Some Twentieth Century Western psychologists have criticized this way of life as being based upon so much fear of suffering, that one simply refuses to live.

The person who would become the *Tathāgata* left home to become a wanderer and to practice those concentrative *jhāna* meditations. He was attracted to meditation and was convinced that it was the path to the end of suffering. He studied under the best teachers in very serious schools where people didn't eat much, meditated all the time, stopped caring about the rest of life and only meditated, so they wouldn't feel any suffering or pain. He followed this kind of schedule for years. At the end of many years he concluded: "It doesn't really help!" He had reached the terminus of the best teaching that the open universities of ancient India had offered, and he hadn't gotten what he was looking for. He became determined to find the truth on his own. But he began his autonomous inquiry from a slightly different angle than anybody had taken before, and this was the start of his breakthrough.

His angle was this: Here is this universe into which we are born. We don't know how it got created. There are many myths, many creation stories, religious stories, but nobody has a clue. All those stories were made up. I don't know how I got here and I don't know how the universe got here. But it seems to me that there must be a way that human beings can understand this universe, fit into the universe, and use the universe itself to teach us how we can get along within it. How can we be happy in this universe? We have to ask the universe what is the right way to live within it. What is the best way to do that? The best way is to just focus upon reality. The reality of this universe will tell us how to live with the reality of the universe, if our questioning is done with authenticity and integrity. But the difficulty is that the universe doesn't speak. Not only that, it's very big. What do you do? You look at the stars; they are beautiful, but they don't tell you what to do. You look at trees or nature or animals or even human beings as part of the universe, but they don't really tell you what to do. His first insight was: to live happily in this world, let's get facts about the world, and from the actual, we will deduce the practical.

His second insight was: we can't interview the whole huge, ancient, aphasic world about how to solve our existential dismay, but my own body emerges "thus" from the universe. My own body is crystallization. If you take sugar and put it in water and you add enough sugar and you put a string in the water, crystals of sugar will congeal around that string. Those crystals of sugar follow the laws of nature. They take their shape based upon the laws of crystallization, basic physics of molecular array, structure, and charge. Our body, the body of every man and woman, the *Tathāgata*'s body, came from the laws of the universe, and crystallized out of the background solution onto a particular string, which gives it shape. In modern language we would say our bodies are based on the laws of physics, chemistry, biology.

The "string" that imparts our unique personal conformation is the molecular code in our DNA. Our body is following universal law. We emerge "thus" from the universe, and inside us, drawing us this way and that way, is the one ancient and eternal truth, the laws that govern things. Two thousand five hundred years later, Albert Einstein echoed the *Tathāgata* by saying: "The most incomprehensible thing about the universe is that it is comprehensible." The mystery of life is not its weirdness, but its lawfulness. Order is stranger than fiction.

So the second insight of the *Tathāgata* was: to sit at the feet of the real, I use my own body as my laboratory. The only thing I can know directly and thoroughly is my own body. The answers to my questions lie within. In his teaching, the word, *loka* means both the "universe", and also our own "fathom-long body." We say, in Western thought, the microcosm and the macrocosm contain the same principles. If we learn truth within ourselves, that truth is applicable to everything. The same laws apply. The American writer, Ralph Waldo Emerson, later echoed this by saying that to know what is true for you today is true for all people and for all time, that is genius.

His third insight, which was an extension of the first, was to proceed via observational neutrality, an empirical take on things. He had a sort of pre-scientific confidence in naturalistic observation, honest receptivity. In order to understand, we need to allow the world to unfold without (as we say in American English) messing with it. Just observe. At this moment in history, meditation took on a new meaning, and became something quite different from merely obliterative concentration. Meditation became the quest for liberating insight. Instead of escaping from our life by concentrating away, meditation became an exploratory inquiry into ultimate truth and its practical implications.

And so he started a meditation practice within his own body, observing it without preconception, as a representation of the entire *loka*, the entire world. The three insights, taken together, upon which this practice was based, can be called the premise of the *Tathāgata*.

The three insights were: from the actual, deduce the practical; to observe reality, one's own *loka* is the best laboratory; neutral, honest, receptivity will reveal nature's insights. From this point, his observations began.

His first observation was that inside the body are many sensations for which there are no words. There were no words in his language and there are no words in our languages today to describe the plenitude of interoceptive vitality, manifesting in the play of sensations that is constantly occurring throughout the human body. We feel a lot of things we can name. We say: "I feel hungry. I have pain in my lower back. My arm itches where I got a mosquito bite." But most of what is going on in our body, we can't name, because language has developed in isolation from the observation of this subjective/objective proprioceptive solar system of the flesh. Our attention is normally turned outward, and we have not developed designations for our perceptions of our inner world. The Dark Continent is us.

The *Tathāgata* began to meditate on the sensations inside his body that took him beyond language, beyond things and nouns. Emerson said, "Every idea is a prison also." Ideas help us orient to the world, but they also confine us by their implicit or even explicit conclusiveness, which then prevents us from open minded, fresh apprehension. Meditation opens out beyond conceptual arrangements, and because it penetrates beyond words, he began to observe new realities in new ways. This led to another observation and another insight. Every time his thought pattern changed, his body changed. Every time his body changed, his thought pattern changed.

With the popularization of psychopharmacology, the so-called Prozac revolution, it has become common knowledge that thoughts require a chemical matrix. If you change your thoughts, the chemical nature of your mind changes. And if you change the chemical nature of your mind, your thoughts change. When people are depressed, if we change the brain chemistry a bit they may feel less depressed. But even more subtly, for example, as I am talking to you, each thought requires a movement of chemical molecules across the synapses between neurons. We have neurons, brain cells, located very near but not quite touching each other. There is a little space between the neurons, called synapses, and when the chemical messenger moves across that space, a thought or feeling can occur. Thinking is physics, chemistry, biology. As I talk with you, you are listening to a chemistry set's slow flow. If you are really listening, your chemistry is being stimulated and altered. Two thousand five hundred years ago, the *Tathāgata* observed: every time I think, there is a change in the flow of sensations of my body. Every time there is a change in the sensations in my body, there is a change in my thought pattern. He got that far by observing his body, just by meditating on it with the pure volition to only observe his somatic sensations and not change anything. He saw mind and body change together. Then he saw, every second, every microsecond, every millisecond, in a time unit smaller than we have language for, everything changes and changes again. Of course, logically we all know that. We live and we change, we grow, our shape changes, our size, our intellect changes, we keep changing until pretty soon we have a whole bunch of grey hair, and start giving lectures on Vipassana. We keep changing, and pretty soon we don't exist anymore.

Things don't change in staggered sequence second by second. The world smoothly remodels itself with unbroken continuity. There is no pause button in the sequence of events causing their subsequence. There is no moment where change is not occurring inside this body of the world.

So, then he realized the whole universe consists of change. Everything is changing all the time. The stars are changing all the time. Every plant is taking oxygen out of the air, photosynthesizing, making green leaves, constant incessant change.

Unlike concentrative escape from reality through meditation that avoids or reconstructs reality according to imposed sounds or images or daydreams, the *Tathāgata* described a meditation the essence of which is realistic apperception of and adaptation to the world from which we thus emerged. Meditation upon reality, closely and systematically observed, revealed nature in new depth.

However, change is not random. There are rules, there are laws. He started with the idea, if I want to understand the laws of the universe, I have to understand myself. I am a representation of the universe. My microcosm represents the universe's macrocosm. It's true that I've gone from being a little baby to having a whole bunch of grey hair. But I didn't change into an elephant. I didn't change into a Belgian. There is lawful change. I am changing according to the laws of human nature. I am changing according to the laws of my own particular nature. So, this great meditator who called himself the *Tathāgata*, observed: "Why do I change? How do I change? How can I find happiness in a self and in a world that are constantly changing? I can't hold on to this body. It is going to change, whether I want it to change or not. I can't hold on to the world. Some day I will disappear from this world; most people don't want that to happen. How can I find peace with the change in my mind and body?"

Later on in his life, he gave another, new definition of the word *Tathāgata*. He said a *Tathāgata* is someone who sees lawfulness everywhere. When I was studying psychology at the University of Chicago, I was taught that Freud invented the idea that the mind is lawful, as propounded in *The Interpretation of Dreams*, and in *The Psychopathology of Everyday Life*. Of course I had to go to India to find out what a Eurocentric concept that was. Two thousand five hundred years before Freud, someone said: everything in the mind is lawful. Everything in the body is lawful. Every thought we have is caused. Every change in our body is caused. A *Tathāgata* sees cause everywhere.

And what causes the thoughts in our mind? Our volitions. Things we want. And what is the pattern of thoughts in the mind? Generally the pattern of thought that you can observe as you are meditating on the sensations of your body, which contains your mind, are two things: "I want something, I'm hungry, I'm cold, I'm tired, I want to go for a walk, I want to talk to my friend, I want to listen to my iPod"—craving for something you don't have that you want. We are adaptive mammals. We shape the world around us by saying: I want this, I don't want this. Give me that, get rid of this. And then along with craving we have aversion. We say, "I don't like it if it's too cold, I'm too hungry, I'm too tired. Change these people; I don't like people of that kind, I want people of this kind." And we are constantly shaping the world to get rid of something we don't want. Craving and aversion occupy most of the mind. And most of the mind is shaping the sensations of flow inside our body. So, the mind and body are very heavily a product of craving and aversion. We live wanting what we don't have, not wanting what we have. The English poet, Alexander Pope, called this, "Light and darkness in our chaos joined . . ."

Even when we're happy, it's simply because some of our craving has been temporarily satisfied. We say it was a beautiful day; it was sunny on the beach. I was with my friends. And there is nothing wrong with that, that's lovely. We have gotten some of our cravings satisfied, but it's destined to disappear. It's not a permanent solution. So, how to be happy when it's not just a lucky day.

Tathāgata came to his next conclusion: If I can observe my body sensations without craving and aversion, then my mind will also be free of craving and aversion. Craving and aversion come from my mind's reactions to my body. But if you learn to just observe your body without craving anything, being satisfied with what you observe, contented with what arises there, in that moment your mind becomes peaceful. And it's a peacefulness that does not require the good luck of a sunny day. Nor does it involve ignoring life by counting sheep or by concentrating on repetitive sounds or prayers. Instead, within your mind, you can sit still, observe your body, and by becoming harmonious and peaceful with your body, you feel focused, alert, in touch with life, and well.

The American poet, Walt Whitman, wrote in "Song of Myself," about wonderful states of mind, of "peace that transcends all understanding." The Vipassana meditation that the *Tathāgata* taught brings peace of mind that is observational, a-conceptual, based on experiential insight rather than mere understanding.

The more that you practice this exercise of meditation on the sensations on your body, neutrally observing them without craving and aversion, the better you get at it. It is a learnable, practicable, reproducible educational meditation for the cultivation of peaceful states of mind.

Now we can see yet one more meaning of the word *Tathāgata*: someone who has arisen in full consciousness as a manifestation of the laws of the universe, who speaks for the universe in impersonally uncontaminated authenticity, who sees the universe as lawful sequences of cause and effect, which therefore can be understood . . . and finally, someone who is free of suffering due to his liberating experiential insight. He is not free of suffering because he has blotted out his mind, or elaborated a benighted delusion, but he has learned the laws of the universe as they apply to human happiness, which is to free yourself from craving and aversion by observing the body in detail with equanimity, and then by living peacefully and harmoniously with yourself and between yourself and others.

The *Tathāgata* started teaching Vipassana meditation initially to wanderers, to people who had left home and were in the free open university. Later on, people who were living in their houses, working at various jobs, came up to him and said: "Please teach us, too." And so his teaching, which started only with holy wanderers, spread to kings, merchants, even to outcasts—people who were considered by others as outcasts; he didn't consider anybody outcast. Ancient India, as most ancient cultures, was patriarchal. In spite of that, he taught women as well. Teaching men, women, rich, poor, young, and very old people on the doorway of death, it is said he "turned the wheel." He set in motion the Wheel of Law. The law of insight, of understanding how the universe is set up to be understood and to be compatible with human happiness.

The *Tathāgata* became more widely known in the West as the Buddha, which means "the awakened person"—a person who is fully awake. Of course, that sounds like he is being contrasted with sleep. "Awake" means he has fully understood, he has fully used his mind and personality to penetrate into the meaning of human life and human happiness.

Although he was sometimes referred to as "a recluse," in the sense that he had abandoned programmed life and become a student, and then a teacher, in the university without walls, he was not at all a recluse in the sense of hiding out alone, avoiding other people or social responsibilities. He was the opposite, a renowned public figure throughout Northern India, a popular star. Autographs were not in vogue then—writing was limited to commercial use—but like any important public figure he was peppered with questions and every attempt was made to have him take up the role of a religious prophet or an advice columnist:

"Hey, you found the meaning of life. You seem pretty smart. Are there Gods? Are there no Gods? Do we float in the sky after death? What happens to our soul? Which rituals will give me prosperity? Who are the chosen people and who are the outcasts?"

He said: "I have no idea. That's not what I studied." People then and today yearn for an organized religion called "Buddhism," which will tell them what to think about politics, what to believe about religion and philosophy. Then and now people try to tease a systematic religion out of the *Tathāgata*'s words. Asking the Buddha questions like: is God in the sky or do we live for eternity, or if we meditate do we live for eternity?" it's like asking the Buddha: "Shall we buy ourselves a PC or an Apple computer?" He didn't specialize in that field. He claimed no tech competence. He specialized in the field of: "How can I live a happy, peaceful, harmonious life compatible with the laws of nature that will free me from suffering". He has been misrepresented as a religious teacher, when he was speaking as an educational psychologist. He taught a way of life that leads to harmony and peace.

Because the teaching of the *Tathāgata* takes no position about mundane things, it endures in a transcultural, timeless zone. It does not grow yellow or crumble with age. It is not on the side for or against the various political issues of any age. It is not owned by a priesthood. The Roman Stoic, Seneca, who had only a veiled glimpse of the Buddha's teaching, grasped its universal essence:

> "We can build a partnership with every age."

It is not surprising that the method he taught is still alive in the world. Here in Belgium there is a meditation center for Vipassana, as there are in many other parts of Europe and around the world. In the twentieth century Vipassana was given a great boost by a very excellent teacher, Mr. Goenka, who has taught so clearly and so convincingly that hundreds of thousands of people have begun to take Vipassana courses in the standardized format that he perfected.

In ancient India, meditation was taught under trees. People would wander up to the *Tathāgata* and say: "How do you meditate? Give me a meditation lesson." Then they would wander off under a tree to sit, with bugs and heat as companions. Today we have a structured ten-day teaching, sheltered in buildings, with step by step clarity every day and from day to day.

A ten-day Vipassana course begins with the taking of moral vows because it's impossible to reduce craving and aversion if all the time you are thinking, "I really would like to murder that son-of-a-gun." Or if you are thinking, "You know, as soon as this Vipassana course is over, I'd really like to get stoned." The whole point of a meditator's life is to be a little freer of craving; it's counterproductive if the whole time you are sitting there thinking, "Everybody must get stoned." The essence of morality is not obedience to imposed vows.

Morality has two profound roots without which the rest of Vipassana is meaningless. The first root helps you be peaceful by your attempt not to be a slave to impulse and whim. Moral positions are tools to calm the mind, to let go of dominance, to "lay down the rod." But moral vows are also ethical. This is the second root. They are rooted in compassion and empathy, pro-social rather than narcissistic values.

There are some books which claim that the Buddha said, "Life is suffering." This is really a misrepresentation of his teaching. The Buddha said: "The world is *dukkha*," and the word *dukkha*, a word from an ancient Indian language means: Nothing is ultimately satisfactory. Because everything is always changing, you can't hold on to anything. So there is always a problem. There is always dissatisfaction. Dissatisfaction—not that the world is always miserable and that we are unhappy all the time. That's not true. If we were always miserable, we wouldn't have attachment to the happiness, which we have in fact experienced. So, it's true there are pleasures in life, but typically our pleasures are based on craving and its fulfillment. You want something and you are skillful and you get. You want a lovely vacation and you are skillful, you earn the money, you go to a beautiful place, you have a nice vacation and that's wonderful. No one is saying there is anything wrong with that. But that vacation passes away. Furthermore you had to work a long time to get that money. And furthermore if you take your vacation in a place like this, it rains all the time.

I was reading about the Americans who came to Ghent in 1814 to sign a peace treaty with England when America was becoming independent. The whole time, the Americans were writing home saying: "Ghent is horrible. It rains all the time. We can't wait to get back to America."

So, even on vacations, you have craving and aversion. When you are meditating, that may well be the first time in your life you feel peace and harmony that is independent from the cycle of craving and fulfillment. You are just sitting there, and initially it's craving and aversion. You begin to work with breathing, just observing, that's all; and suddenly, there is a moment where you are just observing the breath coming in and out. You don't want anything. You don't need anything. You have no problems. You are a totally free human being. That's why the *Tathāgata* was called awakened. Free of suffering; complete; neither needing nor fearing; life, whole and entire as it is—in that second any average person can momentarily glimpse the *Tathāgata*. You are free of suffering. This may last a second or ten seconds and then you start wanting something like: "I want more of this experience," and as soon as you want more of it, you ruin it. Well, there is a big habit pattern of craving.

People ask, "If a person becomes really equanimous like this, doesn't he become a useless zombie? You are happy. This is very dangerous. You don't want anything, how can you participate in a consumer society? The entire American economy rests upon consumer spending." The answer is twofold: Very few people can say they are the *Tathāgata*. All of us continue to have some craving and aversion, and it is unrealistic to imagine that if you take a ten-day meditation course you transcend it entirely. After the course, when you get hungry, you eat; when you get tired, you go to sleep; when you are cold, you put on more clothes; and when you are hot, you wear light summer clothes. We continue to have some craving and aversion, but we are less driven by it, and in particular, the kind of cravings and aversions that are most destructive to human beings are the ones that meditation helps you reduce.

Being cold and putting on a jacket is not a very terrible thing to do, but being angry with people all the time thinking, "I hate this guy; my co-workers are jerks," is destructive. Or thinking, "I have a pretty nice apartment, pretty nice house, but I'm dissatisfied with my life. I should have more recognition. I should have a better car. People shouldn't talk to me in that way, I should have more respect," that kind of craving and aversion eats away at us. These cravings and aversions, which in psychiatry we call psychosocial—the human being in context with other human beings—that's where our most important cravings and aversions are. In meditation you realize everything I want is a fantasy inside of this body. If I were peaceful and happy in my body, if I could sit still and just meditate, without craving and aversion, why would I want all these extras in life? Why would I be so angry? Sometimes people face horrible things, warfare or violence towards their family, but most of the time we are not dealing with that. Most of the time we are living and complaining in our mind, that we don't have what we want, when in fact we have everything we need.

The second answer to that fear of becoming a passive zombie is that when meditation reduces your negative social interactions, you begin to think of ways of helping other people. When we are not filled with craving and aversion, we do not become vegetables. When we are looking at the laws of our animal nature we find that it is intrinsically caring and social. The *Tathāgata* said, "People ask all the time: 'Isn't meditation selfish?'" That was asked back in his days, just as it is asked today. He gave the simile of the birth of a calf. (If you go to India, you can see this happening in the middle of the city. Here in Belgium you have to go to the countryside.)

Cows give birth standing up, sometimes they lay down, sometimes they are standing up and the calf just emerges. The calf kind of plops on the ground and it's covered with the placenta and the birth sack and the cow eats that to get protein back. The calf lies there a short period of time and suddenly it starts to kick, and it stands up.

The cow now has two problems. One problem is she is very depleted, particularly of protein and fluids. Cows get a lot of their fluid from eating grass; they get back protein from actually eating the placenta of a calf and also from eating the grass. So, the cow has to start eating right away. Her life is at risk; it's in a weakened state. The *Tathāgata* said we should be selfish like a cow whose life is at risk. We need to eat every day. We need to take care of ourselves. He did not a teach a path of self-harm or self-sacrifice. When you become free of craving and aversion, it doesn't mean you should stop eating or taking care of yourself. On the contrary, like a cow you should take good care of yourself.

However, the cow has this little calf. This little thing can't eat grass. It needs its mother right away. She has to start nursing it and taking care of it. This cow is responsible for other living beings. The *Tathāgata* said that the proper life of a meditator is like the life of a cow. You take good care of yourself. Human beings are born out of human bodies; that's just our body. But our psyches, our minds, are products of culture. So, we need to start giving right away. As soon as we learn meditation, the first thing that comes up when the craving and aversion lessen is moments of pure freedom—free of craving and aversion, and then we get moments of generosity. How can I do my work better? What work is really important? What can I do to use myself and my psychological freedom to make a better life for other beings? This happens as a spontaneous occurrence as craving and aversion reduce.

There is a final dimension to Vipassana meditation. After the *Tathāgata* had completed his path he thought to himself: "Human life is incomplete unless we have a feeling of reverence and devotion." Most people have a feeling of reverence and devotion for some imaginary man in the sky, but we don't know whether he is in residence. The *Tathāgata* said he felt reverence and devotion for the laws of nature themselves. When understood they bring peace and harmony. The universe is compatible with human beings to be happy and peaceful if they live according to the laws of nature. We should not hold in awe men or gods, but the laws of nature themselves.

Einstein said, many people asked him: "Look, you are a scientist, you are doing all this math, to you the universe must be cold and dead. Einstein, you don't seem to believe in God. You think, the world is just a bunch of rocks following $e = mc^2$. It must be quite boring and you must not have any deep feeling." Einstein replied that the more that he followed the path of truth, the more he found himself "reduced and humbled" at the "grandeur of reason that is incarnate in existence." So, it seems that Einstein and the Buddha had a very similar feeling.

Vipassana is a deeply emotional practice. This law of the universe, which the *Tathāgata* called the *Dhamma*, this Dhamma exists in a way that's good for me. This world of *dukkha* also contains laws whose analogues dwell in me. The deepest inklings of my heart reflect the laws of life. At least some degree of freedom, wisdom, love and joy are built into me, are waiting for me to actualize them out of my own nature. Out of realization of Dhamma springs a reverence for this beneficent and liberating force. An understanding of the way the world works teaches us how to live. The world of *dukkha* is also a world of Dhamma.

A *Tathāgata* emerges as a person, but transcends personality. Losing all personal preferences, all self-referential craving and aversion, the *Tathāgata* speaks from the universal, about realizations that are not limited to any time or place. A *Tathāgata* is a type, a recurring phenomenon, that appeared many times and places in the past, and that will reappear. A *Tathāgata* is a manifestation of Dhamma who can speak it, who can teach it.

The meaning of the word *Tathāgata* is: A person who speaks for Vipassana, which makes us integral with the freedom and opportunity that are also properties of the way things are. How good a day it will be when we too are humbled into awe and reverence by the world just as it is!

Questions & Answers

College of Arts and Philosophy
University of Ghent
December 7, 2007

Q: What's the difference between the kind of meditation you describe and the kind of meditation called Buddhist meditation?

A: When the *Tathāgata* was teaching in ancient India there were many religious practices, but there was no organized religion. There was no such thing as Buddhism. Buddhism came into existence hundreds to thousands of years after the *Tathāgata* died. He called the type of meditation he used, "Vipassana." He never used any term equivalent to Buddhism, which means an organized "ism," a set of beliefs. Instead he recommended Vipassana, a practice, and Dhamma, a way of life. But gradually "Buddhism" developed. There are many practices that are now called Buddhist meditation. I don't know what all of them are. You would have to spend your whole life studying all of them. We don't condemn or contradict them, but they are not the direct, historical connection to the *Tathāgata*.

Q: How is it different from Yoga?

A: Yoga is a set of exercises, attitudes, and philosophies for the promotion of health. It was developed in India approximately six hundred years after the *Tathāgata*. Vipassana meditation, as taught by the *Tathāgata*, is a way of observing natural laws within the laboratory of one's own body, of coming to terms with craving and its impact on personality, and of developing a harmonious way of life. Vipassana is not connected to physical exercises and health treatments. Yoga is not connected to a Buddha. They are old friends these two, and many meditators do yoga to maintain their health. But at the practical level they differ. The transmission of insight, freedom, and reverence, based purely on neutral observation, are the defining features of the *Tathāgata*.

Q: Is the desire to change something in your life, to be able to live more happily, also a form of craving you should free yourself of?

A: Excellent question. It may or may not be. That's a very sophisticated question. Supposing we consider something like a person's studies. You want to change something in your life; for example, you are going to get a MA degree in nursing; or you are getting a PhD in computer science. Is that just craving? The answer is: most complex long-term actions are a mix. Most people don't become entirely free of craving, and probably, if you are, let's say, a student, there is certainly going to be some craving involved. You may well be thinking: "This will earn me more money. I'll have a better career." We are human beings. We are not unrealistic, perfectionistic, or realized saints who take a ten-day course and come out a Buddha. The Buddha described how freedom from craving is a long gradual process, which occurs in many stages. Even many stages of "enlightenment" are accompanied by cravings, but less than before, and with less pernicious effects. The question is: How much craving and how much good volition? What are their relative strengths? I was talking to a Vipassana meditator who is here this evening and he was completing his studies with a nice degree from which he can earn well. He told me how Vipassana had encouraged him to consider also, "What can I do that will most benefit people?" Realistically, some craving is there, but we can adjust our lives very creatively in a way that helps us, but also helps others. It is similar to the cow and the calf. The cow does eat. She does take care of herself. But she is also concerned with the well-being of her calf. We should change our lives so that we are healthy, vigorous, happy, self-caring, good human beings, so that we have more to give. Well-tempered cravings can slowly mature into social virtues. So, I recommend that you neither give up your desire to grow, nor make yourself unhappy with dissatisfaction.

Q: Is meditation a daily practice? And how long do you meditate? Can anyone learn it? How long does it take to learn to meditate?

A: Let's start with that last one. How long does it take to learn to meditate? There are two answers. One is: Vipassana is taught in ten-day courses. So, we say, it takes ten days to learn. But at a deeper level the answer is, it takes either a whole life or many lives! In India, they say you keep getting reborn. So, you may learn best after practicing meditation in many lives! Meditation is an educational psychology. Like any good thing in life, you don't come to an end of it. The things that we can fully accomplish are boring. How long does it take to be a good parent? The answer is, once you have a child, for the rest of your life you are a parent. It keeps changing, and the role of the parent keeps changing. How long does it take to be a professor? Well, in the United States you get a tenure-track professorial position after the PhD. But once you become a professor you don't stop reading. You have to keep studying. We say it takes ten days to learn meditation but it is a lifetime process. You keep learning and growing.

Can anyone learn it? The answer is: Pretty much anyone who can sit still for a longer period of time. Some people may get confused if they spend ten days in silence. They can't follow directions over such a long, private time. Maybe that person will have trouble learning. I would say almost anyone with reasonable levels of human problems can learn. When people apply to our centers, our teachers review every application form and help students decide whether the ten-day course is the right thing for them.

Is meditation a daily practice? Yes, it is. We recommend twice daily practice. Once the person completes a ten-day course, and goes home, they are completely free citizens; we don't have any organized religion. We don't solicit for money. We don't send anything in the mail. I have been a meditator now for over thirty years; I have never gotten a single thing in the mail asking me to give money. Since the courses are taught for free, everybody at the center is just donating their time. The *Tathāgata* taught meditation in the same way that the stars give starlight. They just shine it down for free. It's just a gift of the universe. Similarly, we recommend that after a person takes their introductory ten-day course, they meditate every morning and every evening for one hour each. It sounds like a lot, but if you get to really appreciate meditation, it sounds like a little. You feel it's the best part of your life. Why would I make it less than two hours? So, meditating an hour in the morning and an hour in the evening is a good way to live a life, to walk the path, to become deeply a part of the path of meditation. But it's all voluntary.

Q: You have referred to going back to our animal true nature as changing into a loving caring being. However, it seems that the animal kingdom is everything but loving. Don't we need our psychosocial laws to avoid the animal-like suffering?

A: Yes, I totally agree. When I mention going back to our animal nature, I mean, we learn to observe who we really are. We are biological mammals, and not abstract "mind" or "souls". I love dogs and think dogs are very wonderful beings. But you can't imagine a dog taking a Vipassana meditation course. So, yes, this question is very correct. We do need to activate our human nature or higher nature. There is no way you can meditate without being a respectful, socially aware person. We do not mean to imply that complex social institutions can be dissolved. On the contrary, biologically, we are already complex social beings, like apes and ants.

Q: Could you give some advice on practicing Vipassana during a depression?

A: We advise people to learn to meditate Vipassana by taking a ten-day course. It's the systematic, continuous, unbroken nature of the ten-day course that leads you to actual insight. To get deep insights into your true nature, to really observe yourself, takes time and energy and patience and a bit of perseverance. It's like learning a language. It's hard to learn a language without having some time of immersion. So, can you take a ten-day course if you have depression? We have an application form, and if somebody writes down that they are depressed, Vipassana Teachers will call you or e-mail you and ask you to please tell us more.

The word "depression" is very variable in meaning. If somebody feels very depressed and can barely get out of bed and can't motivate himself to eat, and stays in bed all day, but can't really sleep at night, that's a strong depression. The answer is, no, you shouldn't come to a meditation course, because how would you participate? How would you meditate if you can't get out of bed? How will you understand the discourses? How will you hear the instructions? Even if you hear them, your motivation is so low, how will you follow through on them? So, that's not a good time to come to a meditation course.

At other times the word "depression" is used in a very different sense: "I am depressed. I don't like my work. I think, maybe I should move, but I don't know if I want to move. I am depressed, but I have enough motivation. I am going to work. I am eating. I am sleeping, but I am unhappy." That's the colloquial sense of the word "depression" but it sounds like you could get out of bed in the morning. You could attend the meditation sessions that go on all day. You would have the motivation to work. Sure, you can come.

We help people to assess whether they are likely to benefit from the course or not. Once a person has learned to meditate, we hope that might help them prevent depressions. Of course, we can't predict everything that will happen to a person in life. Maybe somebody will get depressed even if they learned to meditate. And then we hope that they can meditate while they are depressed and it will help them to come out of it. We don't recommend meditation as a treatment for anything. It's a way of life. It's a practice. An educational psychology for everybody. So, we don't recommend it to treat physical or mental illness. But if you know how to meditate and if it should happen that you feel depressed, meditation may remain quite helpful to you.

Q: The world and its nature is a fantastic paradise to live in. A person like myself can easily find peace of mind in this paradise—Wow! However, there comes an aversion when reading about environmental pollution. How should someone think about disturbances of your peace of mind?

A: That's a very good question. Most people, particularly those of us in Europe and North America, find ourselves in a mix of pleasant and unpleasant circumstances. Most of us are not in extreme misery. We are not slaves—there was an article in the *New York Times* estimating that there are ten million people who are enslaved in the world today. Without a certain amount of good fortune it would be hard to meditate at all. On the other hand, even the luckiest of us are beset with problems. There has never been a human being who hasn't faced problems. Right now one of the big problems is environmental pollution. I hope it is on everybody's mind. What about the spread of nuclear weapons? So, in every historical era there are certain problems and the problems change. In the Buddha's era there was warfare. There were big wars in his era. So, although the world looks at times to many of us like a paradise, there are millions of children every year dying of malaria.

The balance of meditation is like this: If I shut out the suffering of others, I become a selfish and sealed-off person. But if everyone else's problems invade my mind and ruin my equanimity, what will I offer to help the troubled world? The *Tathāgata*'s way, the Vipassana way, is to create a private sanctuary, like a university, like mealtime or bedtime. Our sanctuary consists of meditation courses, and twice daily meditation. During those brief times we try to establish deep, independent, inner wells of peace and harmony. All the rest of the time, we are trying to bring out our personal peace to manifest in the world.

Every human being who is capable has both a desire and an obligation to do what he or she can do to help. Different people will pick out different problems. Somebody will say, I am working on civil rights of migrant workers who are held in slavery. Someone else will say, I am working on defeating malaria in Africa. Someone also will say, I want to become a doctor specializing in infectious disease. Someone else will look into environmental pollution. We should actively seek to use the well being that we get from meditation to put ourselves in a position to help with our particular skills, with the particular problems that we have control over, but there is no one living in a paradise that's free of malaria or environmental degradation. On the other hand, rolling in useless anxiety or guilt helps no one.

Freedom means the opportunity to work as hard as you can for what most deeply moves you. Meditation augments freedom, not escape.

Q: Philosophies of psychology say that truth and reality are very complex and problematic notions, and that there are as many truths and realizations as there are people, for there is a structural lack of meaning. But you speak of reality, the meaning of truth. How do you see this?

A: That's an excellent question. Vipassana meditation is a practice of harmony and equanimity, but it is not an answer to all philosophical questions. Vipassana can't answer questions like, is there a god? Or is there eternity? Or what happens to the soul? Or is there a soul? Or what happens when you die? And what is the nature of truth? What is the nature of reality? That's like saying, is it better to buy an iPhone or a Blackberry? Vipassana meditation doesn't comment on that. Vipassana is a tool to gain happiness, or relative happiness, to increase one's happiness, to make oneself a more socially active and useful person, to gain a deeper sense of reverence and gratitude. This is accomplished by observing the body systematically and continuously without trying to manipulate or to change anything. That's the reality that Vipassana is speaking about. It is useful in helping a person to learn how to overcome craving and aversion and to be more peaceful. The definition of reality is a utilitarian definition. It helps the person to make progress on the path. It doesn't answer other philosophical questions and is not intended to do so. Speaking to you as a scientist, I would say that the operant reality in Vipassana is its contribution to well-being, a pragmatic and utilitarian operational definition.

Q: When you speak of the feeling of freedom while meditating, this I suppose is a thoughtless state. When I get in this thoughtless state, I think, I'm in a thoughtless state and then, away goes this freedom. What to do with this problem?

A: I have had this problem about ten thousand times, or more. Well, that's why meditation needs to be practiced regularly for a lifetime. You can't expect to stay in that pure, craving-free moment. Maybe one time it will last for seconds, then you are disrupted by craving or self-consciousness. Maybe another time it will last a minute. The point is not to grasp it. The basic nature of reality is, it's always changing. And as it changes, your thoughts change. So, how can you expect your mental state to not change when the basic thing you have just learned is that everything is going to change? So, you accept the fact that it just changed. But you also accept the fact: "Well, this one passed away. Something new will come again."

Good night!

About the Author

Paul R. Fleischman, MD, trained in psychiatry at Yale University, practiced psychiatry for over thirty years, and has been honored by the American Psychiatric Association for his humanistic and spiritual contributions to medicine. He is the author of numerous articles and books, including *The Healing Spirit: Religious Issues in Psychotherapy*, *Cultivating Inner Peace*, and *Karma and Chaos*, among others.

Paul and Susan Fleischman took their first Vipassana course under the guidance of S. N. Goenka in 1974. In 1998 they were appointed Vipassana Teachers with the responsibility of outreach to professional, academic, and literary audiences. Dr. Fleischman has lectured at colleges, hospitals, medical schools, and other venues, in Asia, Europe, Africa and the Americas.

About Vipassana

Courses of Vipassana meditation as taught by S.N. Goenka in the tradition of Sayagyi U Ba Khin are held regularly in many countries around the world.

Information, worldwide schedules and application forms are available from the Vipassana website:

www.dhamma.org